MW01064330

"FATHER CLARK,"

OR

The Pioneer Preacher.

SKETCHES AND INCIDENTS

OF

REV. JOHN CLARK,

BY

JOHN MASON PECK AN OLD PIONEER.

Entered according to Act of Congress, in the year 1855, by

SHELDON, LAMPORT & BLAKEMAN,

In the Clerk's Office of the District Court of the United States for the
Southern District of New York.

INTRODUCTION

The incidents, manners and customs of frontier life in the country once called the "Far West,"—now the valley of the Mississippi, are interesting to all classes. The religious events and labors of good men in "works of faith and labors of love" among the early pioneers of this valley, cannot fail to attract the attention of young persons in the family circle, and children in Sabbath schools.

The author of this work, as the commencement of a series of PIONEER BOOKS, has chosen for a theme a man of singularly benevolent and philanthropic feelings; peculiarly amiable in manners and social intercourse; with habits of great self-denial; unusually disinterested in his labors, and the first preacher of the gospel who ventured to carry the "glad tidings" into the Spanish country on the western side of the GREAT RIVER.1

The writer was intimately acquainted with this venerable man, who, by all classes, was familiarly called "FATHER CLARK," and induced him to commence sketches for his own biography. His tremulous hand and enfeebled powers failed him soon after he had gotten to the period of his conversion, while a teacher in the back settlements, and he was unable to finish the work.

By correspondence and personal interviews with many who knew Father Clark, and from his verbal narratives in our interviews for many years, the writer has been enabled to give a truthful sketch of the most important incidents of his life.

While seriously disposed persons of every age and station may derive pleasure and profit in contemplating the moral portraiture given, *it is to the young reader, more especially, the author dedicates the memoir of* FATHER CLARK.

CONTENTS

CHAPTER I.

Birth—Ancestry—Misfortune of Becoming Suddenly Rich—A Religious Mother—Fate of an Elder Brother—Mathematics—Purposes of Life—Deportment in Youth—Views of War.

CHAPTER II.

Clark becomes a Sailor—Privateering—His Subsequent Reflections—Last Visit to his Parents—Sails as Mate to the West Indies—Pressed on Board the Man-of-War Tobago—A Fight and Death of the Gunner—Admiral Rodney—Escapes from the Tobago—Visits his Brother—Ships for England—Taken by the Spaniards—Obtains his Freedom, and again Pressed on Board the Narcissus—Deserts a Second Time, and Swims Ashore on James' Island, off Charleston, at Great Risk.

CHAPTER III.

Mr. Clark arrives at Charleston—Meets with Friends—Interview with John Scott—The Story and Fate of Duncan—Alarmed, and Relieved by an Old Shipmate—Stationed on Cooper River—Returns to Charleston—Protected by Three Scotch Tailors—They all Escape—Adventures in a Swamp—Reach Gen. Marion's Army—Clark Proceeds to Georgetown—Enters a Row-galley and reaches Savannah—Sails to St. Thomas—Voyage to New York—Proclamation of Peace—Returns to the West Indies—Shipwreck—Various Voyages—Distress of Mind—Forsakes a Sea-faring Life.

CHAPTER IV.

Retires to the Back Settlements in South Carolina—Teaches a School—Self-righteousness—His Experience for Twelve Months—Despondency—Reads Russell's Seven Sermons—Conversion and firm Hope—Removes to Georgia and Becomes a Teacher there—First Methodist Preachers in that Quarter—Mr. Clark joins the Society.

CHAPTER V.

Appointed Class Leader—Desires to Visit his Native Country—Takes a Berth on the Royal George—Singular Notions on Board—A Storm—Interview with

Tom Halyard—His Conversion—Arrival in London—Sabbath Morning—Visits the Foundry and hears Rev. John Wesley—Parting with Halyard—Sails for Inverness.

CHAPTER VI.

At Moorfield in London—Returns to Georgia—Received as a Preacher on Trial—Richmond Circuit—Testimonials—Character as a Preacher—Walked the Circuit—Views on the Methodist Episcopal Government—Views on Slavery—Blameless Habits—Thoughts on Marriage—Love Cured by Prayer—Gradual change of Views—Contemplates a New Field—Quarterly Conference—Conscientious Scruples—Philanthropy to Negroes—Withdraws from the Conference—Parting Scene.

CHAPTER VII.

Clark Journies towards Kentucky—His Dress and Appearance—Colloquy—Hospitality of Mr. Wells—Recognized by a former Convert—Description of a "Big Meeting"—Persuaded to Stop and Preach—Effects Produced—Mr. Wells Converted—A Revival—Shouting—Family Religion—Departs—The Wells Family turn Baptists.

CHAPTER VIII.

Mountain Range—Manners of an Itinerant—Preaching in a Tavern-house—How to avoid Insults—Hospitality—Reaches Crab-Orchard—Preachers in Kentucky—Baptists, "Regulars" and "Separatists"—Principles of Doctrine—School-Teaching—Master O'Cafferty and His Qualities.

CHAPTER IX.

Schoolmaster Equity in 1796—New Customs introduced—Mr. Birch Discarded—Enrolment—Books Used—New ones Procured—Astonishing Effects—Colloquy with Uncle Jesse—The New School-House—A Christmas Frolic—Shocking Affair by the Irish Master—A Political Convention—Young Democracy—A Stump Speech—New Customs—A True Missionary—Trouble about Money—Mr. Clark leaves Kentucky.

CHAPTER X.

Journey to Illinois—Story of the Gilham family, captured by Indians—Hard fare—Mr. Gilham attempts to recover them—Indian War—Peace made—The Family Redeemed—Removes to Illinois with Mr. Clark—Navigation of Western Rivers—Story of Fort Massac—Terrible sickness—Settlement of New Design—An ungodly race—First Preacher in Illinois—A Stranger in meeting—First Baptisms—Other Preachers—First Church Formed—Manners and customs of the French—Indian War—Stations or Forts Described—PIONEER BOOKS projected.

CHAPTER XI.

Religious families noticed—Capt. Joseph Ogle—James Lemen, Sen.,—The three associates—Upper Louisiana—Attack on St. Louis—The Governor a Traitor—The assailants retire—American Emigration encouraged—Baptists and Methodists go there.

CHAPTER XII.

Forms a Methodist Class in Illinois—Gradual change of Views—Mode of Inquiry—Circumstances of his Baptism—Practical progress in Baptist Principles—Zeal and influence in promoting education—Early Schools in the Illinois country—A formidable obstruction to a pupil—Three fellows in the way—Want of books—A whiskey-loving teacher rightly served—Effects of Father Clark's teaching—Visits Kentucky again—Visits to West Florida—Interview with a Sick man—Efficacy of Prayer—A Revolution.

CHAPTER XIII.

Baptists, "Friends to Humanity"—Their Anti-slavery position—Mr. Clark joins them—Manner of his reception—His Views of African Slavery—Views of African Colonization—Made Life-member of a Colonization Society—Circulars on Slavery—Personal behavior—Conversational Gifts—Writes Family Records.

CHAPTER XIV.

His mode of Traveling—Excursion in Missouri, 1820—His monthly circuit in Missouri and Illinois—A night Adventure—A Horseback Excursion—Origin of Carrollton Church—Faith and Prayer—Interview with Rev. J. Going—A "Standard" Sermon—An Affectionate Embrace—Comforts of Old Age—Last Illness and Death.

SKETCHES OF "FATHER CLARK."

CHAPTER I.

Birth.—Ancestry.—Misfortune of Becoming Suddenly Rich.—A Religious Mother.—Fate of an Elder Brother.—Mathematics.—Purposes of Life.—Deportment in Youth.—Views of War.

Cast your eyes, reader, on a map of Scotland. Look towards the north-eastern part, and you will find distinctly marked, the *Frith of Murray*, a narrow channel of salt water, like a bay, penetrating a long distance into the interior of Scotland, and named after the Earl of Moray, or Murray.

Follow up this channel to the city of Inverness, once regarded as the capital of the Scottish Highlands. Near this city is the small and secluded parish of *Petty*, which we notice as the birth-place of Father Clark, on the 29th of November, 1758. Here his father, grandfather, and other ancestors, for several generations, were born, lived and died. A brother of his grandfather, whose name was *John Clark*, became an eminent scholar, and taught the parish school for many years. All the family connections, for many generations, were strict Presbyterians, who paid careful attention to the morals of their children. The classics and mathematics, the Presbyterian catechism, and their forms of religious worship were taught the children in the parish schools, and in families, in that part of Scotland. They were taught to do justly, love mercy, and always speak the truth.

The father of our John Clark was named Alexander, who, in the early part of his life, owned and worked a farm. He had a brother named Daniel, who was educated for the ministry in the Presbyterian church; but he had no taste for that business, and became qualified for a merchant. In this capacity he sailed for South Carolina; then went to Georgia in company with some Scottish traders by the name of Macgilvary, who monopolized the trade with the Creek Indians. In that connection he gathered a large fortune, and dying, left his estate to his brother Alexander, who had previously married a respectable and religious woman. They had two sons, Daniel and John, and three daughters, one of whom lived many years after her mother's death.

The fortune of Daniel the elder proved the ruin of the father of our hero. He neglected his farm, kept open house for his friends, drank intoxicating liquors freely, lived in a style of luxury and grandeur, gave his name and credit on the notes of his companions; loaned his money to sharpers, and in a few years was reduced to bankruptcy. He lived to old age, and after a long period of intemperance and wretchedness, was reclaimed and died a penitent, past the age of three-score and ten.

The mother of John Clark became a very religious woman, and taught him to pray in early childhood, and that he was a sinner against God, and must have his heart changed, be converted and saved through Jesus Christ. Before he was eight years of age he had many serious impressions about his salvation, many alarming fears about death and hell, and thought he experienced a saving change at that early period of life. He often declared to his Christian friends, that to the instruction and prayers of his mother at that tender age, as means under God, he

11

was indebted for his salvation. And rarely have we known a man more earnestly devoted to the religious instruction of children and youth. It would come out from a gushing heart in almost every sermon, and by kind and gentle hints and friendly expostulations leave a deep impression on every family he visited.

His elder brother Daniel was a moral and amiable youth while under the charge of his mother; but he was sent from home to a grammar school at an early age. He became an excellent scholar, was taught the mercantile business, went to Jamaica where he soon became rich. But he lost two ships, taken by privateers in the war between Great Britain and the American Colonies, became disheartened, gave way to temptation, and followed the footsteps of his father by becoming intemperate, and died a bankrupt and a miserable drunkard in the 37th year of his age.

John Clark's father knew the benefits of a good education, and spared no pains or expense in providing his children with the best means of instruction that Inverness could afford. John was sent to school at the age of five years. He read the Scriptures and other English books before he was seven; and at that period was put to study Latin. He learned the grammar, read Corderius, and studied the elementary classics for two years; but he disliked the study of Latin and Greek, for which he often sorrowed in after life. During this time he was at a boarding school, away from home and all the kind influences of his affectionate mother.

"All these circumstances," he writes in the sketches before us, "laid the foundation for an invincible prejudice against the acquisition of that useful language;—useful because much of the English tongue is derived from it. Also it disciplines the mind, corrects desultory habits, and forms a taste to imitate in oratory and composition, classical authors. I think it highly necessary for those, who aim at common education, to memorize a Latin vocabulary. Study mathematics to discipline the mind, and study well our English classic writers.

But my early and deep-rooted aversion to the dead languages prevented me from receiving much advantage from Latin and Greek authors, so that I acquired but a smattering knowledge of those languages."

When his father learned his aversion to classical studies he sent him to an excellent school in the parish of Nairn, to learn arithmetic, book-keeping, mathematics and natural philosophy. The purpose of his father was to qualify him to join his brother in the mercantile business in the island of Jamaica. At this school he studied geometry, trigonometry, mensuration, surveying, astronomy, and navigation in all its branches.

Two objects occupied his youthful mind, and which he craved in all his studies. They engaged his thoughts by day and flitted through his dreams by night. They were the only airy castles his fancy ever built. First, to spend about eight years on ship-board, and visit foreign countries and see the manners and customs of other nations. And, secondly, then to settle for life in one of the American colonies. With his mind fixed on these objects, with a steadiness of purpose that never tired, he entered on those studies connected with navigation with an eagerness and zest rarely equalled in youth. He could not divest himself of this propensity to a sea-faring life for the period proposed. He had no inclination to be a mere sailor, or to spend his days with the profane and drunken of that class of men. He saw enough of such specimens of degraded humanity in the port of Inverness to excite feelings of disgust and sympathy. In all his longings to be on ship-board, his benevolent nature sympathised with the heedless and wicked sailors. He would often retire and weep over their miseries, and think of plans for their reform and relief, when he should attain the command of a ship.

During the period of youth, Clark was singularly amiable, moral, kind-hearted and generous. He lost no time by idleness, had no inclination to the vain amusements and frivolities of youth, and sustained an estimable character for personal sobriety, good order and morality. The unfortunate example of his father excited pity and disgust; the devoutly religious character of his mother confirmed and deepened the impressions of childhood. There was more of puritanical strictness, form, and rigid orthodoxy, than active piety and the outpourings of the religious emotions, in the Church of Scotland at that period, and young Clark neither felt nor manifested those feelings of ardent love to the Redeemer, and comfortings of the Holy Spirit, that had been awakened in his young heart at the early age of eight years, or which distinctly marked his religious character in after life.

Our youthful friend became an enthusiastic lover of liberty and of the rights of man, at an early age, and which continued the ruling passion during life. In the period of old age he records these facts.

"When I was very young, I deeply imbibed the spirit of war—owing chiefly from hearing much of the success that attended the British arms by land and sea, during the war in Canada. When in the seventeenth year of my age, the Revolutionary war between Great Britain and her Colonies commenced, and I soon found myself as much opposed to the spirit of war as I was formerly in favor of it."

This feeling remained after he became connected with the navy, and caused him to desert the service, into which he had been forced by the press-gang. And yet, as if to show us that a young man so amiable, kind-hearted, and philanthropic as Clark, was far from perfection, or even consistency of character, he engaged in the business of privateering; a business now regarded by civilized nations as barbarous and immoral.

CHAPTER II.

Clark becomes a Sailor.—Privateering.—His Subsequent Reflections.—Last Visit to his Parents.—Sails as Mate to the West Indies.—Pressed on Board the Man-of-War Tobago.—A Fight, and Death of the Gunner.—Admiral Rodney.—

Escapes from the Tobago.—Visits his Brother.—Ships for England.—Taken by the Spaniards.—Obtains his Freedom, and again Pressed on Board the Narcissus.—Deserts a Second Time, and Swims Ashore on James' Island, off Charleston, at Great Risk.

The propensity of young Clark to a sea-faring life remained ungratified until he was twenty years old. Much as he desired to see the world, and repulsive as was the conduct of his father to his sensitive feelings, John had no wish to run away clandestinely—to leave his affectionate mother and sisters, or to reject the monitions of his conscience. He patiently waited until the proper time should come; until he attained the period of manhood, and could go with his parent's blessing. And then, even filial affection and true philanthropy, prevailed over a churlish and selfish temper, and prompted him to regard the welfare of his parents to his own personal interests.

It was in the summer of 1778, in the twentieth year of his age, that John Clark embraced the opportunity of carrying into effect his darling purpose of life, by engaging in the transport service. But to this he was induced by higher motives than a selfish indulgence. His education had been completed, and he had spent some time copying in the town and county office of Inverness. To the close of his life he wrote in a style of uncommon neatness and accuracy. This employment furnished no income beyond ordinary expenses. The extravagance and dissipation of his father, had nearly reduced the family to want. The riches realized from their uncle Daniel's estate, gained doubtless by fraud and extortion, from the Indians of Georgia, had made themselves wings and flown away.2 The farm in Petty was left, but the income was barely sufficient for their support, and nothing can prosper under the management of an intemperate husband and father; and John piously and resolutely resolved to do his best in the business of his choice, to keep their heads above water.

He embarked in the transport service, at low wages.3 Finding, on his return, that his father's extravagance was fast wasting away their means of support, and hoping to obtain in a more speedy way the means of relief, he went to Greenock and entered on board a privateer; and the voyage was so successful in capturing two valuable merchant vessels, that in less than a year he returned home with his wages and share of the prize money, amounting to more than $200. Of that business then regarded lawful and honorable in war, fifty years after, he writes thus:

"This unchristian, inhuman, and almost piratical practice, was never permitted in Scotland before that war. But my moral feelings by this time began to be impaired, for my situation in life deprived me of the company of the godly, and 'evil communications corrupt good manners.'4 Although my conscience recoiled at doing that which I was not willing others should do to me, yet I made necessity my excuse, and pleaded the example of those who I then thought knew more and were better than I was."

After remaining with his parents a few days, and leaving all the money he could spare, for their use, he gave them the parting hand, and in accordance with a promise made with one of the owners of the privateer, he entered as mate one of the prize ships taken, called the Hero, for a voyage to the West Indies. There he intended to join his brother, and engage in business with him.

Little did he anticipate this was the last parting time with his parents, but let him tell the story.

"I shall never forget the morning I left them. My mother, who loved me most tenderly, when we parted, expressed, with the greatest confidence, without shedding a tear, that God would preserve me by land and by sea, from every danger. My father walked with me about one mile to a small river where I had appointed to meet a young man with a horse for me to ride to Port Glasgow, near Greenock, where the ship was to fit out; and as we parted, my dear old father wept like a child. Very likely he had forebodings he would never again fix his paternal eyes on me, for he was infirm, and his constitution much broken by intemperate habits. This was in May, 1779, and he died in the autumn following. I left my friends mourning, while I went away rejoicing; for though I intended to follow a sea-faring life for a few years, I fancied it was in my own power to see them whenever I pleased. I little imagined that man may appoint, but God may disappoint.

"I went on my way merrily, without the least thought that Unerring Wisdom had set the day of adversity over against the day of prosperity, to the end that man should find nothing after him.[5] According to my engagement, I shipped with my friend, the owner's son, on the Hero as second mate, from Port Glasgow, to the Cove of Cork in Ireland, where we waited for a convoy. There we were joined by a large fleet of victuallers, store ships, and transports, with one or two regiments of Hessians, for the port of New York. Our vessel and some others was bound for the West Indies. We set sail under convoy[6] of the frigate Roebuck, of forty-four guns. The convoy and transports were destined for New York, and we that were bound to the West Indies sailed in company to a certain latitude, when we parted, and were then under convoy of the Leviathan, of seventy guns, and a sloop of war of sixteen guns. Then I began to notice and examine God's marvellous works in the boisterous deep. Nothing transpired during the passage worth relating until we got to Barbadoes, and there I was pressed on board the Tobago, a British war vessel of eighteen guns. Here ended my prosperity and adversity came. Or shall I say this seeming affliction was a blessing in disguise, intended by Infinite Wisdom for my everlasting good?

"My wages on the Hero were forty-five dollars, for which I sent an order to my mother that she might receive it. Although my mother out-lived my father seven years, I afterwards learned with great satisfaction neither my father nor mother suffered for want of the necessaries or comforts of life while they lived; for many years after I learnt my mother left upwards of sixty dollars of the wages I had sent her."

Mr. Clark was now a sailor, pressed by arbitrary authority on board the British man-of-war, Tobago, and lying in the harbor of Carlisle, in the Island of Barbadoes, to prevent American and French privateers from plundering the plantations in the bays and road-steads of that Island. This business was against all his principles and feelings; for in all his longings for a sea-faring life, it never

15

entered into his calculations to serve on board a man-of-war. Let him give his own views and feelings:

"I was continually unhappy while in the navy, and would have ventured my life to have obtained my former liberty. I made an unsuccessful attempt to escape the night before the ship left Barbadoes, but was detected, and both my feet put in irons, and a sentinel placed over me, with a candle and a drawn sword, the whole night. Next morning the ship weighed anchor, and steered on our course. Great Britain was then at war with three maritime nations, and we suspected every ship that passed, especially if alone, to be a cruiser and an enemy.

"Before night we espied a ship bearing down towards us, when our ship prepared for action. The boatswain blew his pipe, and hoarsely bawled, 'All hands to quarters, ahoy!' My irons were taken off, and after a severe reprimand, I was ordered to my post. When we came within hailing distance, we found the ship to be the Venus, a British frigate, and passed, after giving and exchanging three cheers."

They were about three months lying off and on, upon cruizing ground, in the Caribbean Sea, very short of provisions. Their butter, cheese, flour, lard, and fruit, failed entirely, and much of the time they were on short allowance, when they joined the fleet lying at St. Lucia. The force consisted of two squadrons, one commanded by Admiral Parker, the other by that truly pious Admiral Rolly, as Clark denotes him. The French fleet lay at Martinique, not far distant, but were too numerous and powerful to risk an encounter. So the British lay in the harbor, with springs on their cables, waiting for a reinforcement, and fresh supplies of provisions and naval stores. The French were waiting to be reinforced by the Spanish fleet and land-forces from Hispaniola, (now Hayti,) and both united, purposed to invade the Island of Jamaica. The British Government, knowing the precarious situation of that valuable island, made every effort to send relief, but they were hard pressed by the war in the American Colonies, and they needed an energetic, and skillful commander, to save their West India possessions.

They had a naval officer of great skill and courage, but he had been absent many years on the continent of Europe. This was the celebrated Sir George Brydges Rodney, who had distinguished himself in the West Indies, in 1761, by the capture of Martinique. He was an admirable commander in the navy, but while on land, was profligate, and had wasted his estate, and become hopelessly in debt. In this situation he left England to reside on the continent of Europe. His biographer says, "He injured his finances in a contested election for Parliament in 1768." The French government made some overtures to him, which would have repaired his fortune, but he rejected them with indignation, and remained true to his native country.

Such was the alarming state of affairs in the West Indies that the government called home Sir G. B. Rodney, paid his debts, redeemed his estates, and gave him the chief command of the fleet in the West Indies. This policy, probably, prevented Jamaica from falling into the hands of France or Spain.

Admiral Rodney, with a reinforcement, joined the fleet at St. Lucia; and, as Clark says, "It was the best equipped squadron I ever saw."

Rodney soon captured a Spanish squadron, and used the prisoners with great humanity. This became known to Charles III., the venerable king of Spain, and he issued orders to his naval and military officers to treat all British prisoners humanely.

The arrival of Admiral Rodney at St. Lucia, was the occasion of great joy in the fleet, which had been penned up there for many months, and the French in turn were blockaded in the Island of Martinique, and could not join the Spanish fleet in Hispaniola. While Rodney was watching the French and Spanish fleets, the Tobago, on which our friend Clark had been forced by a press-gang, was ordered to Jamaica with despatches in all possible haste. On this voyage Clark narrates an incident deserving a place in this little work.

"We had a venerable man on board our ship for chief gunner, who, from some unknown cause, had taken a dislike to me, and never gave me a kind word. One beautiful, moonlight night, while sailing near Hispaniola, it was my turn at the helm, and I was astonished at the unexpected behavior of the gunner to me. He approached me with as much respect as if I had been his superior in rank or station. Had he been an intemperate man, I should have accounted for his conduct, as some men are remarkably good natured while under the influence of liquor, and others are very cross and surly. But he was a moral man and never became intoxicated. He appeared in his conversation like a person who had done with this world, and in kind and respectful language gave me a sketch of his life. He had been in the British navy forty years; but the subject on which he dwelt with the most feeling was the bursting of cannon in action; and expressed with an emphatic tone of voice, he had never known a gun "expended"[7] but that a gunner was expended with it.

Next day after dinner as we were sailing near the same Island, an armed brig popped out from the Island and gave us a chase. Our business required haste, and we could not stay merely to fight, and we endeavored to decoy her near by housing our guns. Suspecting our manœuvres, she fired two guns, and altered her course. We, in turn, intended to fire a broadside soon as we could bring our guns to bear. But, alas! the sixth gun we fired burst, and mortally wounded three men, and maimed several others for life.

Our venerable gunner had one foot entirely cut off, and the other hung by his leg. The surgeon told him, he could not survive, and he called for his mate, and told him to adjust his temporal affairs with the Board of Admiralty, and with great composure of mind, and in hope of mercy, he yielded up his spirit."

This incident made a lasting impression on the mind of Clark. The manner of his approach the preceding night, the long and somewhat religious conversation he held, the premonition he seemed to entertain of the approaching calamity, and his sober, orderly and correct life left the fixed impression that the gunner was a Christian. A young man had his skull fractured by the same gun, and Clark stood by and saw the surgeon trepan him, while he exhibited the greatest degree of fortitude and patience. The wounded men were all sent to the hospital in Jamaica, where this youth died.

The fleet they had left behind under Rodney soon had an opportunity to act on the offensive. The French fleet that had been blockaded were reinforced by Count de Grasse, and made an attempt to join the Spanish fleet. They were followed by Admiral Rodney, who sunk one of the largest vessels and captured five others. For this act of naval heroism, he was created a baronet, had a pension of two thousand pounds sterling per annum settled on him by the crown, and at his decease in 1792, a monument was erected in St. Paul's church, London.

The Tobago, on which Clark was, needing repairs, she was hove down for the purpose in Port Royal. In consideration of his fidelity and good conduct after his attempt to desert, Mr. Clark was promoted to the station of quarter-master. This did not reconcile him to the war, nor to the despotism of the officers, and the sufferings of the men on board of a war vessel. He was still resolved on escaping the first opportunity, for as he had been forced on board a man-of-war, in violation of his rights, he thought it no wrong to escape the first opportunity. In company with two other young men he escaped one night, and reached Savannah La Mar, a port on the south-western part of the Island. Here he found a ship taking in lading for London; and so weak-handed, that they scarcely had men enough to heave the anchor. Clark and his comrades were employed at once and helped load the ship; and in great haste to be off, or the time of their insurance would expire. "Here," he states, "for the first and last time in my life, I worked on the Sabbath for double wages."

When the Captain paid off Clark and his companions, he used a stratagem to induce them to work the ship to England. The wages then were forty guineas and forty gallons of rum for the voyage; but John Clark had resolved to visit his brother, according to a promise he made his mother when he parted with her, and no high wages or other inducement would tempt him to break his promise. The Captain professed great generosity, and proposed treating Clark and a young man who was to be his traveling companion, to French brandy; and as Clark suspected with drugged liquor, in order to detain them. He drank but little, while his comrade praised the liquor and took it freely. They had not proceeded far before the young man's legs gave out, and they were compelled to stop at a strange house till next morning. During the night, the young man was robbed of all he had, and being destitute, Clark, as a genuine sailor, and benevolent withal, divided his purse with his unfortunate friend. And he moralizes on it in this language:—"So here I saw the fruits of Sabbath-breaking and trifling company." But on looking back on the events of providence from the pinnacle of three score and ten, he says:—

"I now find that it was the interposition of a particular providence of Him, who is loving and mindful of all his creatures, that the forty guineas and forty gallons of rum, and the French brandy made no impression on my mind to induce me to alter my intentions, and especially my promise to the best of mothers."

He learned at a later period, that though the ship got to her place of rendezvous, yet before the fleet was ready to sail to England, it was overtaken by a most furious hurricane, and the ship he aided to load, was stranded, about a quarter of a mile from the beach. The cargo was lost, and the wicked Captain and every sailor on board perished. Clark adds, "So fatal was that storm on that ungodly people, (the inhabitants of Savannah la Mar,) that there was scarcely as many left, as would bury the dead in proper season."

Mr. Clark traveled across the Island to find his brother, and then went to work to obtain money enough to purchase decent clothes, before he would venture into the presence of his brother, who lived in a decent family, and was much respected. He earned money, but Providence seemed to frown on him, for he lost it, and all he had. So he says, "I resolved at last to see my brother, just as I was in my tarpaulin dress, as sinners ought to come to the Saviour, without any righteousness of their own."

After informing his brother of his career, he blamed him much for leaving the navy; for the education he had and the position he attained would have insured his promotion, and he might have obtained wealth and dignity. He soon found there was no employment he could obtain at Montego bay, and be near his brother, unless it was that of book-keeper on some plantation, and that was an unprofitable business. His brother had become addicted to intemperance, and seemed to be following the course of his unhappy father.

While waiting and undetermined what to do, a Letter of Marques belonging to Glasgow came into Montego bay, and Mr. Clark engaged as a hand, and set out for his native country.

All now seemed encouraging, and he felt thankful to God that he should soon see his parents and sisters again. But while sailing in the Gulf of Mexico, the vessel was attacked and taken by two Spanish frigates of superior force, and the crew were carried prisoners to Havana, in the Island of Cuba. Here Clark remained a prisoner of war nineteen months. Formerly the Spanish authorities treated their English prisoners with great cruelty, but since the humane regimen of Admiral Rodney and the orders of the King of Spain, already noticed, their treatment was kind and humane. But to be confined in a prison, though provided with wholesome food and other necessaries, was by no means pleasant; and the time wore away slowly.

A cartel being arranged, Clark and other prisoners were liberated and soon on shipboard.[9] With gladsome hearts and active hands, they heard the boatswain sing out, "heave O!" as the anchor was raised and the sails unfurled to the winds of heaven; and soon they were ploughing the rippling waves towards a land of freedom. The wind proved favorable, and in a few days they were at anchor off Charleston, outside the bar. Here the good fortune of Clark was again reversed. The eye of an infinite Providence was fixed on this man; his steps were mysteriously directed in all his wanderings, and it was needful he should pass through other and more severe trials, until as gold well-refined, he should be fitted for the Master's use. Mr. Clark expected to be landed in a maritime port, and have eight days allowed him to choose a vessel and berth. But an hour had not passed before a recruiting officer and press-gang were on board, and poor

Clark and several others were again *pressed* on board another man-of-war by British authority.

Surely there is no condition of servitude so galling to humanity, and so directly a violation of human rights, and so subversive of rational liberty, as the infamous press-gang in the British navy. We rejoice that the just and humane sentiments of the age, have mitigated, though not entirely removed, this odious form of despotism in the British government. Through the operation of such oppression, Mr. Clark found himself on board the Narcissus, of twenty guns, and most unwillingly held in the service of George III. Read his own remarks on the subject.

"Now, I was more determined than ever to obtain my liberty. The love of liberty is implanted in our very nature, and nothing can supply the lack of it. We fared well on board the Narcissus; we had the best of fresh meat when it could be obtained, besides butter, cheese, plum-pudding, and a pint of Madeira wine for each day, but all that could not supply the lack of rational liberty.

"The people of the slaveholding States ought to consider this well; for the spirit of liberty is like a magazine full of powder. If it takes fire, it will consume all within its reach, and the danger increases daily. Many slaveholders sincerely conclude that if they work their slaves moderately, clothe and feed them well, the slaves ought to be contented, but Scripture, sound philosophy, and experience—yes, my own experience—prove such arguments to be sophistry. For although I fared on board the Narcissus as well as I could reasonably desire, yet I was more discontented than ever. So I found the old saying verified,—"

'Feed me with ambrosia;
Wash it down with Nectar;
And what will it avail, if liberty be wanting.'

My desires for liberty and peace were so great, that death or liberty was the constant language of my heart."

About this time the British evacuated Savannah, and the Narcissus was appointed a convoy to the transports that moved the refugees from that city to St. Augustine. After performing this duty, the ship returned and lay off Charleston again. Orders were issued to sail to New York, and the night previous Clark and his mess-mates were employed in making preparations for the voyage.

After being discharged from duty, and while at their mess, John Scott and John Clark were invited to join another mess and take grog. The proposal was then made to Clark and his messmate, to obtain their liberty that night by swimming to James' Island, it being from one and a-half to two miles distant. The plan was arranged by Clark to strip in the bow of the ship, all but their trowsers, and swim at first straight ahead in a quartering direction, until they could no longer be seen from the ship, and then turn in the course of the island. He was chosen to take the lead, and he dashed ahead in the direction he had chosen. The others made some delay, as Clark was to turn on his back and wait for them. He found, on trial, the salt water so dashed over his face, that he was compelled to swim for his life. His situation became extremely perilous; the rippling waves dashed in his face and he began to despair of life. And now he became alarmed at the prospect of immediate death, and his sins rushed on his conscience to that degree that even in the perilous condition he was, he dared not to pray for deliverance. The prayers of his mother seemed to ring in his ears, and in his disturbed imagination the spray that beat upon his face were her scalding tears. Like flashes of lightning his sins pierced his conscience, and the terrors of the law, like peals of thunder, rolled over his sinking soul. Such were his views of his sin and guilt, while swimming for his life, that he dared not pray, lest his cries to heaven for mercy should provoke the vengeance of an angry God to sink him in the deep. But let him tell his own experience from his journal at this terrible crisis.

"I expected to launch into the presence of a frowning and sin-avenging God, whose tender mercies for many years I had trampled under my ungodly feet;—I had broken many promises of amendment;—a yawning hell seemed moving from beneath, at the ocean's depth, to meet me on my sinking. Human language cannot express the agitation of my mind, and such was my perturbation for a time, that my strength failed me to such a degree that I could hardly keep myself from sinking. I would willingly have sunk, but the thought of dying without the hope of mercy, was so terrible that I resolved to swim as long as I could keep my head above water, or until deprived of my senses, or till some greedy shark, of which the harbor was never clear, should devour me, and put an end to my struggling."

The impression of dying under the curse of God's violated law, thrilled through his nerves like an electric shock, and he felt in an instant increased vigor, and swam with greater ease. He could not see the land, and when despairing of deliverance, he found a ship at anchor about 200 yards from him, and two miles from any other vessel, and hope inspired his heart and nerved his arms to further effort, and he resolved to board the vessel, knowing that some of the sailors would give him clothes and help him to land. But all was still. Both officers and men were on shore, or in the city of Charleston. He found an old, ragged, and greasy shirt, and a small boat moored to the ship, but conscience demurred: "How can you be guilty of such iniquity, of taking other men's property, when God has wrought such a deliverance?" But reason responded: "It is no more than I would cheerfully allow others to do to me under a change of circumstances."

He got into the boat with the least noise possible, cast her loose, and sculled toward the land. A light breeze springing up he hoisted his oar for a mast, the old shirt for a sail, shipped the rudder and sailed for James' Island. After tying the boat so that it might be found by the owners, he crept into a hay-stack and rested till morning. After waking, much refreshed from the fatigue and exposure of the past night, Clark sought a position where, undiscovered, he might watch the movements of the Narcissus. At sunrise her morning gun boomed over the waters, and with joyful emotions he saw the signal hoisted for her departure. The wind was fair, and the dreaded ship was soon under weigh, and was soon out of sight.

CHAPTER III.

Mr. Clark arrives at Charleston.—Meets with Friends.—Interview with John Scott.—The Story and Fate of Duncan.—Alarmed, and Relieved by an Old Shipmate.—Stationed on Cooper River.—Returns to Charleston.—Protected by Three Scotch Tailors.—They all Escape.—Adventures in a Swamp.—Reach Gen. Marion's Army.—Clark Proceeds to Georgetown.—Enters a Row-galley and reaches Savannah.—Sails to St. Thomas.—Voyage to New York.—Proclamation of Peace.—Returns to the West Indies.—Shipwreck.—Various Voyages.—Distress of Mind.—Forsakes a Sea-faring Life.

At that time transport ships were collecting in the harbor, and waiting to carry off the troops, for the British were about to evacuate the town. This was in 1782. James Island, where Mr. Clark got on land, is a large island south-east and opposite Charleston, across Ashley river, and is separated from the ocean by Folly Island and a channel between; and has several other islands contiguous. Clark says, after noticing the departure of the ship:—

"The next thing that occupied my mind, was, how I would get to Charleston, and what would I do there? I thought that with an old, greasy and torn shirt, and a pair of trowsers as my only covering, every one would take me for an idiot, or at least a worthless vagabond. Could I have seen then as I now see, the hand of HIM who makes sparrows, ravens, lions and other creatures objects of his care; and that all his dispensations towards the children of men are tokens of his paternal love, and means to instruct us;—that without HIM we can do nothing;—if I had then seen these things as I now do, I might have enjoyed peace with God, and been delivered from all tormenting fear. But I was blinded by unbelief or I should have known that what I had experienced the night before of the goodness of God in my preservation would have inspired me with hope for the future."

He soon found a negro hut where he obtained food, and was told he could get a passage to Charleston in a fishing boat. All this time Mr. Clark knew nothing of the fate of his four comrades, who he was confident had followed him, and who, he supposed, were in the ocean, or in nautical language had "gone to Davy Jones' locker." He was taken in a fishing boat across the wide river, and landed at the upper wharf, which he regarded as a providential favor, for it gave him opportunity to keep out of the way of the officers of the navy, and find amongst the common sailors some old shipmate who might aid him in his necessities. He found sailors, in great numbers, at every wharf, and there were many ships taking in lading for British ports, expecting the war would soon close. The great men of France, England, and the United States, were then arranging terms of peace.

Mr. Clark continued his tour along the wharves until he almost despaired of seeing any one who would befriend him. When almost at his wits' end, he espied three men putting tobacco into the hold of a vessel, and to his astonishment and joy he knew them; for many months before, he and his mess-mate John Scott had showed them what they thought was a great favor. It is a peculiar trait of sailors to be grateful, and never forget an act of kindness. But let the interview be in his own language.

"I made towards them with quick steps, and a gladsome heart. I found they were gentlemen indeed, though at first they did not seem to know me. Their disinterested generosity exceeded any thing of the kind I ever met with before. They clothed me from head to foot, and gave me refreshment.10 I then went into the hold, to assist the second mate to stow away tobacco. I was not long engaged in that business before I heard the voice of John Scott on deck—my mess-mate, who I supposed was drowned. I concealed myself as long as I could, while listening to his conversation; for he was narrating the tragical story of the death of John Duncan and myself to the captain."

We will give John Scott a chance to tell his own tale, as recorded from the memory of our friend John Clark.

JOHN SCOTT'S STORY.

"The men who proposed the hazardous undertaking to me and my mess-mate, John Clark, set out from the ship after him, but in a contrary course from mine. One of them, after swimming about one hundred yards, concluding he could not hold out to reach the shore, returned and got on board without being discovered. Another swam about one hundred yards further, and found he would fail, hailed the ship and was taken up by the boat. But I and John Duncan held on our course about half way to the land, when Duncan began to fail; and the last words I heard him utter, were, 'Lord, have mercy on me.' I got to the island, but entirely naked, except a silk handkerchief around my waist. I then ran up and down the sand beach to keep warm till day-light, when I walked on the island and came to a large brick house, where a lady stood in the door-way and directed me to the barn, where a British sergeant lay, who gave me a pair of trowsers, and the lady sent me a fine, ruffled shirt, and a half-worn beaver hat, and gave me a hearty breakfast."

Scott got a passage to Charleston on a fishing boat, for which he paid two dollars; so it seems they weighed his purse by his fine clothes. While John Scott was narrating the desperate adventure, and how two of the number got back to the Narcissus, and Duncan was drowned, with sobs and tears he mentioned his dear mess-mate, John Clark, who, he doubted not, had perished, or been devoured by a shark, for though an excellent swimmer, he could never reach land in that direction. "And here," said the generous-hearted sailor, "is the purse he knit and gave me, and I am determined to keep it as long as two meshes will hold together; for he was the best friend I ever had."

Clark could listen no longer, but called out JOHN SCOTT, while the tears like rain drops, gushed from his eyes, as he sprang on deck, and in a moment the two shipmates, each supposing the other dead, were in each others' arms! They

23

now pledged themselves to each other, never to part, but to live together like brothers. But it is not in man that walketh to direct his steps.11 They heard of a Captain Kelly, who was fitting out a privateer and wanted hands. On application for berths as privates, they learned he wanted officers, and would take them as lieutenants. Clark was deficient in practice, and Scott lacked knowledge in the art of navigation. After some further consideration they went on board the privateer, and to their satisfaction found one of their former fellow-prisoners engaged as surgeon. They now thought they were provided for and should be contented, but before they were ready to sail, a ship of war came into the harbor, with a full description of the deserters from the Narcissus, and orders to search every vessel for them. This so alarmed Clark and his mess-mate that they were at their wits' end. At this crisis Clark fell into the company of an old shipmate by name of John Stewart. They had been captured in company by the Spanish frigates and were messmates while in prison in Havana. Stewart advised Clark to take a berth on an armed sloop, employed as a guard ship, and stationed in Cooper river, a few miles above Charleston. What became of his friend Scott we learn no more. They separated and probably never met again on earth.

Mr. Clark now felt his mind relieved from the fear of recapture, but the respite did not last long. For wages he had nineteen dollars per month, and a complete asylum from the dangers to which he had been exposed; plenty of good rations, and very little to do; so he had two-thirds of his time to improve his mind, which he did not neglect. But God had wise and gracious designs to accomplish by him, and his measure of afflictions was not full. His rest was of short duration, for the sloop was ordered down to Charleston to undergo repairs. There he was peculiarly exposed to apprehension as a deserter, and knew not how to escape detection. But the Friend of mankind provided another asylum, as unexpected as his former deliverances. Connected with the remnant of the British army that still occupied Charleston, were three Scotchmen, brothers, who came from his native district. They were tailors, and employed in altering and fitting the military clothing, so as to suit each person. With them he became acquainted, and they concealed him until they were about to be shipped off with the regiment to New Providence. They told him, in confidence, their parents lived in North Carolina, that the time of their enlistment had nearly expired, that they disliked the army, and desired to escape to a country that was now free. Finally, they entreated Clark to procure a boat, and take them across Ashley river; and if he wished to accompany them, to obtain a man to row the boat back to Charleston. This was a providential opening for Clark to escape, and he engaged his friend Stewart to help them off.

At eight o'clock at night, Clark, the three tailors, and Stewart as boatman, were on the water, and hailed by every ship they passed: "Boat ahoy—what boat is that?" Clark regularly responded in the true marine accent, "Guard-boat;" and thus they escaped unmolested. The last ship they passed ordered them to stop and come on board, but they kept on directly towards the margin of a large swamp that lay close by the river. They intended to turn up the river when on the border of the swamp, and land on dry and firm ground above. After considering themselves out of danger, they leisurely plied two oars, while Clark sat in the stern and steered. Not a word had been spoken by the party, until one of the men broke silence in a low but emphatic tone, "Lord, have mercy on us—there's a boat close on us—put ashore—put ashore!"

Clark instantly put the boat towards the shore, struck the muddy bank, and all plunged into the swamp but Stewart, who turned down stream. A palmetto swamp, when covered with water, is a horrible place in day-light—what must it have been to these wretched wanderers in a dark night! What the boat was after that alarmed them, or who manned it, they never learned. It might have been sent from the last ship who suspected the "guard-boat" was not its real character; or it might have contained a party of runaways like their own; or some of the native inhabitants might have made a stealthy visit to town.

Mr. Clark and his friends were frequently up to their knees in mud and water, and tearing their clothes and skins with the rough palmetto leaves. The Scotch tailors were excessively frightened, quite panic struck, expecting every moment to be made prisoners; or perhaps shot down in the swamp. The grass was higher than their heads, and they could not see five yards distant. Clark allayed their fears by assuring them there was no danger from soldiers or marines, for no person, unless insane, would attempt to follow them in such a swamp. He urged them to keep together while he led the party. After a terrible struggle, they got across the swamp about four o'clock in the morning. Next day they secreted themselves in a thicket and rested till night, and then traveled on a south-western course by the direction of the stars. They knew the camp of General Marion was somewhere in the pine barrens, and steered their course in that direction. Next day they were so far within the American lines, they ventured to call on the inhabitants and found them truly generous, and were made welcome and comfortable. The day following they reached Marion's camp, reported themselves as deserters from the British in Charleston, and were received by the heroic General and his men with true politeness. Next day the three Scotch tailors applied for passports to North Carolina, and Clark for one to Georgetown in South Carolina, which were readily granted. Though the war had practically ended, peace had not been proclaimed, and every thing was in an unsettled state. Mr. Clark reached Georgetown, sixty miles north of Charleston, but found no employment there. The British had evacuated the place, but the inhabitants were left destitute, and subsisted on rations furnished by the American army, and every thing was in confusion. Being almost destitute of clothes and money, Mr. Clark engaged for a short voyage on a coasting vessel, and came very near being captured by a British whale-boat. It was only by a desperate effort they escaped. Soon after returning from that trip, an American row-galley, with thirty oars when she had a full complement of seamen, came into port. She was armed with swivels, muskets and cutlasses, and bound on a cruise to Savannah. As the boat wanted seamen, Clark obtained a berth on board. On their voyage they lay by one night at Bull's Island, and in the morning found two British whale-boats lying near, and all hands fast asleep. The Americans fired a musket and halloed to arouse them, but as it was understood the war was over, neither party was disposed for a fight. So they parted in peace. The American boat staid at Bull's Island another night, to see that the British boats did no injury to the inhabitants, and then went to Savannah.

By this time Mr. Clark had become heartily tired of war on both sides, and his conscience was reproaching him for engaging in such exploits; he was continually unhappy, for God was calling him to enter his service, and like Jonah he was trying to escape. But he felt it to be his duty to obtain the means of subsistence, and a Sweedish neutral vessel from St. Thomas, being in Savannah, he shipped on board and sailed for that island. As the vessel belonged in that port, all hands were paid off and discharged. The captain, who had taken a fancy to Clark, offered him the post of mate if he would sail with him, but the mate had treated Clark with so much friendship, he would not take his place. The mate, Clark, and several hands, made arrangements to lodge on shore with a Mr. Campbell. The town of St. Thomas was a neutral port, and ships from five nations, who had been at war some years, were frequently in the harbor. To prevent collisions among the sailors of these different nations, especially when intoxicated, and to preserve peace and good order, the town authorities required each seaman who lodged in the town, to obtain a license from the officer who had charge of that business. Mr. Campbell told Clark and his comrades if they were in bed by nine o'clock, they need not apply for a license. But they found their host was mistaken, or else he purposely deceived them. Though all were in bed and perfectly quiet, they were aroused up by the police, sent to the fort, and amongst hosts of fleas, and heaps of filth, were kept until ten o'clock next morning. And then they got released by paying fines and costs at the rate of about twenty dollars per head, for a most wretched night's lodging.

Next day they went to Tortola, a small island that belonged to Great Britain. Here they shipped on the Peggy, a vessel bound to the port of New York, and laden with rum and sugar. Clark's friend was first mate, and he was made second mate. His friend left the ship at New York, and our friend John Clark, who was amply qualified, was advanced to the post of chief mate. While they lay in the harbor of New York, peace was proclaimed, and Clark, though an officer on board a British merchant vessel, on the day of public rejoicing could not resist the impulse to unite with the Americans in their shouts to Liberty. He felt thankful to God that though he had been forced sorely against his will and all his notions of the rights of man as a creature of God, to perform service on board of British war ships, he had never been compelled to fight that people who were contending for their just rights, and whose banner was freedom. The truth is, Mr. Clark was innately and by conviction, a true republican, and an enemy to oppression in every form.

The vessel in which he was now second in command, took in a cargo of lumber and sailed for Tortola, where they loaded with a cargo of wine and West India goods, and again sailed for New York. A terrible storm drove them ashore near Cape Hatteras, off the coast of North Carolina, where the vessel was lost, but the crew and cargo saved. Cape Hatteras is the extreme point of a long low island that separates Pamlico Sound from the Atlantic ocean. From North

Carolina he made a voyage to Cape Francois, now Cape Haytien, in the island of Hayti; from thence to Charleston in South Carolina, thence to Jamaica and back to Charleston. Nothing special occurred in these voyages in which Mr. Clark had the berth of first mate. He now made some preparations for a voyage to London, but he was a very unhappy man, and had been, at times, since his escape from the Narcissus. We will hear his own story.

"'Twas now the Spirit of HIM who died on the cross to save sinners, that alarmed me continually with an assurance that I should never see the face of God in peace unless I quit the sea-faring business. I resolved to go into the country and teach a school, where I could have opportunity to read the Bible, meditate, and attend to the salvation of my soul. My conviction and repentance increased to despondency, and I now found no difficulty in refraining from the use of ardent spirits, which had been growing by long habit, until it had become truly alarming. Before I met with this distressing but gracious and salutary change, I was a willing slave to sin and Satan; but now I was still a slave, but a very unwilling one. I have believed for many years that there is an important difference between being awakened and being penitent. A person who is thoroughly awakened and does not repent, is filled with tormenting fear, which may be the beginning of wisdom."12

CHAPTER IV.

Retires to the Back Settlements in S. Carolina.—Teaches a School.—Self-righteousness.—His Experience for Twelve Months.—Despondency.—Reads Russell's Seven Sermons.—Conversion and firm Hope.—Removes to Georgia and Becomes a Teacher there.—First Methodist Preachers in that Quarter.—Mr. Clark joins the Society.

It was early in the month of March, 1785, that Mr. Clark, after much struggling of mind and conscience, came to the determination to quit the seas and become a religious man. The captain and hands were anxious he should remain, and make the voyage with them to London. The only defect they perceived in his character as a sailor and officer, was, his desponding temper, and singular habit of being much alone. None of his friends knew the nature of his troubles; none could sympathize with him; and had he known himself and the true nature of the Christian religion, he might have exclaimed with the ancient patriarch, "Miserable comforters are ye all."13 But he then had no clear views of gospel truth, nor how a holy and righteous God could justify and save a sinner consistent with his law which saith—"The soul that sinneth, it shall die."14 But he can best describe his own case in the language he left in the sketch before us.

"I have already mentioned being afflicted with that tormenting fear that precedes repentance, and which is unspeakably great. Had I then known as much of the gospel as I now do, I need not have made such mistakes as I did, nor suffered the hundredth part I was made to suffer. For I firmly believe that when an awakened sinner can say with all his heart, 'God be merciful to me a sinner,' like the publican,[15]; or with Saul of Tarsus, 'Lord, what wilt thou have me to do?'[16]; or in the language of one of our sweetest hymns,

'Here, Lord, I give myself away;'Tis all that I can do;[17]'

he is then in a state of salvation, though he may not have received the spirit of adoption.[18]

"I had been in great distress as a sinner, off and on for more than two years. At times I would be in the greatest distress, and have a horror of conscience beyond description, and then it would wear off and I would return to my sinful courses. The first of my permanent conviction was while in the port of Charleston in March, 1785, after I had engaged to make a voyage to London as second mate, when I became continually alarmed, lest if I went to sea another voyage I should never see land, nor the face of God in peace; my day of grace would be past. In this awful distress of mind I obtained my discharge, and under this salutary but distressing conviction, I set out for the back settlement of South Carolina. On Saturday I came to a tavern house near the Eutaw Spring, and told the family, I made it a matter of conscience not to travel on the Sabbath, and wished to tarry with them till Monday. But they misunderstood my case, and got some of the neighbors to watch the house on Sunday night; imagining I was a robber, and had accomplices to aid in robbing the house. But I did not blame them, for I felt deeply my wickedness against God, and appeared to my self worse than any robber on earth.

"On Monday morning I fell in company with some backwoods people, who had been to Charleston and were going to Fishing river settlement on the frontiers. Both parties soon became well suited; for I wanted to teach school, and they wanted a teacher. They treated me kindly, and I went home with them, and in a few days a school was made up, and I engaged to teach for them one year. I now endeavored to abstain from every appearance of evil, read the Scriptures, and prayed in secret several times in a day. I was so far from knowing the gospel method of salvation, that, notwithstanding the instruction given me in childhood, from the Bible and the Presbyterian catechism, I sincerely thought that true religion consisted only in outward reformation of conduct. My moral and serious deportment surprised my employers, who were irreligious and not over much righteous. They thought it very singular that a man who had followed a sea-faring life, should be so humble and religious, and often spoke of it. But they no more comprehended the state of my mind, nor understood my case than they could lessons in Latin, Greek, or Hebrew.

"I spared no pains to attain to the highest degree of self-righteousness, and really thought that would stand by me in the great day of final accounts. Yet notwithstanding all my efforts, my besetting sins would return upon me with all their force. The more I strove to be righteous, the stronger it seemed my sins grew; and what is always an inseparable companion, despair tormented me to such a degree that my life became an intolerable burthen. After hearing my classes read in the Old and New Testament, I often went out of my school-house to weep and pray. I would go into a thicket, throw myself on the ground and cry for mercy; yet for a twelve month I was trying to prepare myself that I might deserve mercy. No pen can describe the horrible temptations that beset me, and the sore trials that I experienced. My whole life seemed to me to have been a series of the vilest actions, words and thoughts imaginable. I had agreed to board round with the scholars, but Mr. Andrew Love, a generous, kind-hearted gentleman, offered to board me gratis. This gave me more time for reading, and opportunity for retirement. At times, I thought I was so bad the Almighty could not have mercy on me; and then it seemed as if a curse hung over every thing I set my hand to do. It seemed to me at times it was an imposition on the people for one so wicked, as I regarded myself, to attempt to instruct the youth. I could blame no person but myself. My life was a burden, and I often wished I could be annihilated.

"It is a most laudable custom with the pious Presbyterians where I was brought up, for all the family that can read, to spend the Sabbath, when not at Church, in reading the Scriptures, and some good religious book. But I even thought it wrong for such a sinful person as I was to look into a good book; and such books were very scarce in Fishing river settlement. I made inquiry for such books, and one of my employers sent me 'Russells's Seven Sermons.' I ventured to read the discourse on the sin against the Holy Ghost, though with a very trembling heart. But the happy change that came over my mind tongue cannot express. It was the mere glimmerings of hope that through Jesus Christ there was mercy for me. I now felt a degree of reconciliation to God that I cannot describe. I knew before my heart was enmity against God, and at times I felt angry that God would not have mercy on me. I was now astonished beyond expression how I could have had such feelings, and what had become of my sinful nature. My past sins, which seemed to be unpardonable, were gone, and it seemed that nothing but love to God and man had been left in their place. Although I had been taught from my infancy the doctrine of salvation through the merits of Christ, yet I never before believed truly in his divine merits and gracious intercession, but held on to my own righteousness; and yet I was rationally convinced I had none, and I learned by bitter experience I could get none by my own working."

Mr. Clark now enjoyed peace of conscience and faith in the Lord Jesus, yet for some time he did not know this was a state of salvation. He had learned this lesson, that no man can say that Jesus is the Lord but by the Holy Ghost.[19] But it was several years after, as he grew in knowledge and the grace of our Lord and Saviour Jesus Christ,[20] that he became established in faith and hope, and for more than forty years, he had no doubts of divine acceptance.

The inquiry was once made of a shrewd, old Scots divine, "What is the *best* evidence of a gracious state?" The prompt reply was, "Forty years close walk with God." Our old friend gave this evidence and something over. According to his own narrative which we have copied, his experience of a great and gracious deliverance from the bondage of sin (which he always ascribed to the mighty agency of the Holy Ghost,) took place in March, 1786; just one year after he left ship-board in Charleston. He lived to the autumn of 1833; the period of more than forty-seven years; and during the whole time, without any drawing back, he exhibited daily living evidence of the wonderful and gracious change he experienced. He was remarkable for meekness, humility, and godly fear, and yet he never expressed a doubt of his adoption.

We do not find in his narrative any account of religious meetings, or that he heard any one preach for more than a year; nor can we find any evidence of any church having been organized in this remote settlement, by any denomination. His school, which had been a large one, closed a few weeks after he met with the change by which he passed from death to life. About that period the country south of the Savannah river, now in the middle part of Georgia, was new, and attracted the attention of a large immigration from Virginia, and Mr. Clark supposed the work of surveyors would be in demand. He thought he might obtain a contract, and then look out and purchase land for a farm and settle down for life. But he piously observes, after nearly half a century had past away, "The Author of all events had a higher and more responsible calling than any that occurred to my mind, and that was to preach the gospel."

He went to Georgia, to the country on Broad river, a branch of the Savannah, some where in the region of the present counties of Elbert, Wilkes, Oglethorpe and Madison, then all new, and to which immigration was rapidly tending. But he found no demand for surveying, and again took up a school, near Colonel Wootten's residence on Broad river. A school was raised in the following manner. The teacher, after consulting some of the heads of families, and learning the probability that a sufficient number of pupils could be obtained to justify the engagement, on his part, drew up an article in the neatest style of penmanship he could, forming a contract between himself and the signers; he engaging to teach the branches named, at a certain rate per quarter, and they engaging to pay him a specified sum at the close of each term. The subscribers would put opposite their names the number of scholars they engaged to pay for, and if they sent more, the expense would be in proportion; if less, they were still bound to pay their subscriptions. A popular teacher would soon have a third more scholars than at first subscribed. This mode of contract for teaching the common English branches has been almost universal through the south-western States, and prevails to this day. In some instances two or three persons will make a contract with a teacher, and bind themselves to pay a salary, and then look to their neighbors to aid in making up the school.

The school houses, if that term be applicable to the most inferior of the whole race of "log-cabins," were constructed of rough, unhewn logs, with a chimney of sticks and clay at one end; the door-way in front, and the shutter, if it had one, made of split slabs or boards. A log cut out of one side left an aperture for a window, and a slab placed under it, running the length of the room answered the purpose of a writing-desk. The floor was of earth and seldom cleansed. The surrounding forest, in the border of which this rough cabin was located, furnished ample supplies of fuel, and a spring of water near poured out the refreshing and primitive draught for the thirsty pupils.

About the time Mr. Clark began his school, as he states,

"Two Methodist preachers, by name of John Major and Thomas Humphries, formed a circuit in those parts, and preached at Col. Wootten's house, where I boarded. They pleased me so well that I joined them."

Turning to the Minutes of the Methodist Conference, we find the names of these ministers placed on the Georgia circuit for 1786.[21] Their labors were abundant and efficient, and several societies were formed in that part of Georgia.

CHAPTER V.

Appointed Class Leader.—Desires to Visit his Native Country.—Takes a Berth on the Royal George.—Singular Notions on Board.—A Storm.—Interview with Tom Halyard.—His Conversion.—Arrival in London.—Sabbath Morning.— Visits the Foundry and hears Rev. John Wesley.—Parting with Halyard.—Sails for Inverness.

We are unable to give anything very definite about the religious employment of Mr. Clark while he remained in Georgia. He was prompt and gifted in prayer-meetings, and before many months was appointed class-leader. We never learned when he commenced regular preaching. Without a license he gave exhortations in the prayer-meetings; but his private conversations were probably the most effective means at that period in bringing sinners to Christ.

Gradually, and with many misgivings, on his part, his mind became impressed with the duty of preaching the gospel to his fellow men. He was meek, modest, humble, and thought far less of his gifts than others did. His sensitive conscience shrunk at undertaking a work for which he felt so poorly qualified, and we suppose he did not appear before the public as a preacher until after his return from his native country. His amiable temper, courteous manners, and kind feelings, without any effort on his part, gained him the confidence and good will of all with whom he held intercourse.

It was not more than one or two years after he joined the Methodists that he resolved on a visit to his native land. He had received the avails of teaching for several terms; his dress was plain, cotton homespun, and cost but little; and his board had been gratuitously bestowed by Colonel Wootten. It was a beautiful morning in April that he led for the last time, by the solicitations of his host, in the family devotions, and after breakfast, and again singing a favorite song, he gave the parting hand to each of the family, white and black.

"I'll go with you, brother Clark, to the forks of the road," said the venerable Colonel. As they walked along the lane, Clark thought, though kindly repulsed before, he would again tender payment for his board and several articles of clothing he had received as gratuities, and he mentioned the subject as they arrived at the junction where they must part. "No, my dear brother," said the kind-hearted old Methodist, "you have done a heap more for my family than they can ever do for you. For until you talk'd to that wayward boy, our George, who was wild like, and had been after cards and whiskey, I felt orfully afeared he would be lost and ruined te-totally. But when I know'd you'd tuk him in hand, and I'd he'rn you pray so all-graciously for him in the tobacco house, I sort'r pluck'd up heart, and concluded my poor prayers for him would'nt do no harm. So I prayed too as hard as I could. An' now he's so steady and cheerful, and sings so pretty sin' he join'd Society.—O, brother Clark, I hate to part with you; but do pray for me and mine, when you're on the great ocean;—and should you ever get back ag'in to Georgia, remember my house's your home, as long as I live. And ef George lives and holds out as he's begun, he'll never let you want, for I do believe he loves you better nor his father and mother."

The old Colonel was full and he could say no more—his heart was gushing out of his eyes like a shower of rain, as he gave the hand of Mr. Clark such a parting squeeze as caused him never to forget this old Methodist brother.

He might have paid his passage and gone in the cabin of one of the slow sailing vessels of that period, which were usually from two to three months in crossing the ocean to Europe. But though he never knew the feeling of avarice;—though he never hoarded up money for its own sake, but believed steadfastly in the same providence that clothes the lilies of the field, and feeds the birds of the air, he went aboard like a true-hearted sailor, before the mast. Arriving at Charleston, he found the Royal George, a trim, snug, merchant ship, just fitting out for the port of London, and shipped as a regular seaman.

The wind proved fair, and for some weeks the weather was favorable;—then a terrific storm overtook them which lasted three days. Clark manifested due courtesy with his shipmates, and showed prompt obedience to the officers. The Captain eyed him closely, but during the storm he found him to be a prime sailor, and that he understood both the theory and practice of navigating a ship. The sailors in the forecastle thought he had queer ways, but all concurred in the opinion of the Captain and mates that he had smelt salt water before; and yet he was singular.

When he first came aboard, they spoke of him as a "green 'un;" "a land-lubber." "He might do to punish *grub*, but he'd never do in a storm."

The storm came on, and Jack Clark, as he was called, was found to be the best hand in the mess to work ship. He could run up the shrouds and out on the yard arms, like a monkey; hold on with one hand and take in a reef with the other in the quickest time. From the captain, whose keen look was on him as he walked the quarter-deck in sullen dignity, to the cabin boy whose laughing eye watched the new hand; all perceived he was a regular "old salt;" and if he had commanded a ship, as some one intimated, he had never crept in at the cabin window.

32

But he was a strange fellow, for when grog time came John was seldom seen coming for his allowance. When fair weather came, and the sailors lay about the deck sunning themselves, and spinning long yarns, John Clark was reading in his berth. Thus days and weeks passed away, with the usual monotony of an old fashioned sea voyage.

"What book is that Jack Clark reads so much?"—said one old salt to another as several hands lay basking on deck one day. "It's the BIBLE," was the reply from a pale looking sailor, who had just got out from a sick-berth, "for he read a long yarn out of it the other day to me." "Hurrah," shouted a wicked and witty fellow, who was listening;—"Is—Jack—what d' call 'em—a PARSON?" "I don't know about that," said pale face, "but I think there are not many parsons about Lun-nun that know more about the Bible than Jack Clark. And I can tell ye more, shipmates, he can *pray* too, and make his prayers as he goes along without the book; for I he'rn him not long sin'." "You he'rn him pray!" shouted two or three voices in quick succession. "A sailor *pray*, and that without a book? Well, that's more than the parsons can do."

The sailor who had let out the secret of John's praying, was in a serious mood. He had taken a kind of sailor prejudice to Clark when he first came aboard, and manifested no disposition to be on terms of intimacy. This sailor, whom we will call Tom Halyard, (having forgotten his real name) had been sick for several days, and was neglected by his shipmates,—even those of his own mess, except Clark, who nursed him, obtained from the cook a little nourishing soup, and showed so much sympathy as to spoil all his prejudices and win his confidence. There is nothing like sympathy and kindness to work one's way into the heart's core of a true sailor. Taking advantage of a convenient interview in private, when he was beginning to recover, Clark had a long conversation with this man on personal religion, and the way of salvation through Jesus Christ.

Thomas Halyard had a pious mother, who in giving him some of the formal lessons prescribed by the English church, talked to him about his state by nature as a sinner in such a way as no one but a mother can talk. Tom's mother died when he was a little boy. His father was a profane drunkard, and cared nothing for godliness, and hated God-fearing people. His repeated acts of outrage and abuse of the poor motherless boy, drove all filial feelings from his heart, and made him disgusted with his father's brutal manners. He ran away while quite a youth, and went on board a ship. He soon learned the habits of a sailor, and could swear as profanely and drink as full an allowance of grog as the best of them in the ship. Yet there were moments when the image of his mother, and especially her dying words to him, and prayer and praise to God, would come with power on his memory. He had once been sick when he was a little child, and his kind mother nursed him, placed her hand on his feverish brow, and spoke words of kindness and love in his ear, which he could never forget. The kindness and conversation of Clark, during his recent illness, had broken through the crust that the world and a wicked life had encased his softer nature in, and unsealed the fountain. Tom wept like a child as he lay in his hammock, and listened to the simple teaching of his brother sailor, and heard him read lessons of instruction from the Book of God.

John Clark told him some thing of the history of his own life, how he left the man-of-war and swam ashore, and how God mercifully preserved his life in that perilous adventure. But when he told him how the Lord brought him to see his wretched state as a sinner, and the wonderful deliverance and joys of pardoning mercy in the interior of South Carolina, and the new life he since lived;—all was so strange and wonderful,—so unlike any thing he had heard before, and with all so touching, that the tears rolled down the weather-beaten cheeks of this tar; he sobbed aloud, and before he was aware of the scene he was enacting, John Clark was on his knees beside his hammock, praying in an audible, but low, musical voice for his salvation. No wonder the sin-struck sailor thought John could pray better than the parsons could with a book. True, he knew very little about parsons, for he had followed the sea more than twenty years, and during that time had seen "divine service" performed on land not half a dozen times. Sometimes he heard the burial service read by a captain over the mortal remains of some shipmate, who had been sent to "Davy Jones' Locker," over the ship's side.

From the time Mr. Halyard disclosed the character of John Clark to the crew, he was treated with particular respect. Wild and wicked, and as little disposed to knock off drinking and swearing, and put on religion, all respected their shipmate John Clark. The officers found out the "cut of his jib," and treated him accordingly. Sailors find out the peculiar traits of human nature quite as soon as any class. Had Clark put on a sour face and assumed the airs of a religious man; had he been unsocial and moody, and reproved them in a harsh and unkind tone of voice, and in presence of others for their drinking, swearing and frolicking habits, and taken pains to appear peculiarly righteous, he would have seen trouble. They would have regarded him a graceless hypocrite, and treated him with contempt and persecution. He gave them no direct reproofs, and yet his manners and intercourse, courteous, kind and winning, impressed their consciences more than a hundred moral lectures would have done. They feared him, respected him and even loved him.

The voyage finally wore away, and they were in the port of London and safely moored, on Saturday; after sailing up the river Thames from its mouth at the Nore, about forty-five miles. At that period London was a great city, though since that period, its population has more than doubled; its fine houses and long, winding streets have extended, and its blocks and squares, have gone far out into what was then open country. Boarding-houses for sailors were then a horrible "den of thieves," and the abodes of intoxication and other infamous vices. And, even in this age of philanthropy and reform, there are numerous places in London and all other large seaports where decoys are employed to entice the newly arrived mariner to places where he can be filched of his money, his senses and his life. But Christian philanthropy has hoisted the Bethel flag, as the signal where sailors can worship God in comfort and peace, and boarding-houses have been established as places of virtue, good order, temperance and comfort for this

34

useful class of humanity. John Clark had no inclination for accommodations in houses of infamy, and Tom Halyard seemed very much inclined to follow his example.

Sabbath morning came; the sun shone dimly through the smoke and haze of a London atmosphere, and the sailors generally were making preparations to desecrate the Lord's day by their customary visits to rum shops and infamous houses. Mr. Clark had risen early and performed the service required of him as a sailor, put off his tarpaulin dress, and appeared on deck with a smiling countenance, in a neat and cleanly suit, having, as the sailors said, the "cut and jib of a land-lubber." One of his shipmates cried out,—"halloo, Jack,—whither ahoy now?" "I'm going to find a place to worship God, with his people." Clark lingered on deck for a few moments on the Sabbath morning, when Thomas Halyard appeared in his Sunday suit, rigged out in real sailor trim.

"Where away now, Tom?" enquired one of the sailors, while he cocked his eye at another, with the true sailor leer, and rolled his quid from one cheek to the other. "Only going a short voyage on land with Jack Clark"—was the response, in a serious tone.

"I'll be harpooned if Tom Halyard is not a-going to turn parson," said one. "Not yet," replied another. "Tom was on the sick list not long since, and thought he was bound for kingdom come;—and Jack Clark physicked the old boy out of him, and he's now going to chapel to pay off old scores." "And I'll tell you what, shipmates," said another, "we've all been bad enough to be keel-hauled, and John Clark and Thomas Halyard are as good sailors as I ever wish to mess with. 'Spose we follow them and hear what the parson says to-day?" "Agreed," said several voices, and away they went up the street, headed by Clark and Halyard, who walked lovingly arm in arm.

It became a fixed principle in the mind of Mr. Clark, at that early period of his religious history to follow as Providence led; or, which was the same thing to him, after a season of prayer for divine direction, to follow such impressions of his own mind as appeared to spring from a truthful and right source. Neither he, nor his companion knew any chapel in London, or where to go;—but they walked on in a friendly manner. Mr. Halyard asked questions how they were to conduct themselves in church, and Mr. Clark described how the meetings were managed in Georgia.

They had passed through several streets, when Mr. Clark saw a man walking in the same direction, and ventured to inquire if he could direct them to some chapel where the gospel was preached. "And it's being afther the gospel ye would be axing? Well, it's mesel' that answer ye, for I'm a going there mesel'—'Tis to the Foundry ye'd like to go?" Clark replied they were strangers in London, just from ship-board, and wished to find some church where they could hear the gospel. The honest Hibernian with whom they had come in contact, was a zealous Methodist, then on his way to the "Foundry," in Moorfields, where the celebrated John Wesley established his regular meetings in 1739. This venerable patriarch of Methodism was still there, and though fourscore years old, preached on the occasion of the sailors' visit. Mr. Clark had heard of the achievements of Mr. Wesley, from the preachers in Georgia, and it had been among his warmest aspirations to see and hear this distinguished divine before his return to America. It was a singular providence that guided him to the Foundry chapel the first Sabbath he spent in London. The scene was almost overpowering, and he listened with rapt attention and drank in every word the preacher uttered.

Halyard wept profusely, though on board ship, and before his illness, and Clark's conversation, he had been singularly hard-hearted. No distress could bring a tear from his eyes.

The other sailors behaved with decorum. The scene was new to all. None before, except Mr. Clark, had ever known a "parson," as they called all ministers, pray without a book, or preach anything but a written or a printed discourse. Whether any lasting impressions were made on their companions is not known; but Halyard was an altered man, and one of the "first fruits" of John Clark's labors.

They spent the day at the Foundry; some of the generous-hearted, christian brethren shared with them their lunch, and invited them to attend class-meeting in the afternoon. The next week they obtained their discharge from the ship, and Thomas Halyard went into the country to find some distant relatives, and John Clark entered a coasting vessel and sailed along the coast of England and Scotland, and up the Moray Firth to Inverness, on his way to his native parish.

Mr. Clark had not heard from his surviving friends for several years. He learned the news of the decease of his father when he visited his brother in Jamaica, but his mother and two sisters were then alive and well. No mails were then carried across the ocean, and it was a rare thing that opportunity presented to send a letter. He had written two or three letters while in the sea-faring business, but he knew not whether they ever reached their destination; and they were never received.

A mixture of the most pleasurable and painful emotions agitated his mind as the rough hills and mountains of his native land hove in sight, and the schooner on which he engaged to work his passage, entered the estuary of Moray Firth. And as they passed Nairn, where he attended the boarding school and studied the sciences, his feelings became overpowering. The scenes and incidents of youth, and his airy visions of a sea-faring life; the wonderful providence of God that led him in a way that he knew not, preserved him amid a thousand dangers, and brought him back to his native hills, were so oppressive that he could no longer look on the hills and vales around him, until he had retired, wept heartily and offered a prayer of thanksgiving to God for his mercies that endureth forever.

Coming again on deck as they slowly sailed with a light breeze up the Firth, towards the mouth of the river Ness, every feature of the landscape appeared natural and familiar. There in the distant perspective were the alpine mountains of Scotland, as range on range exhibited features of the wildest grandeur. Again, as they approached the city, his eye caught the aspect of the rich lowland country lying along the Ness and Spey rivers. Here was a maritime landscape scarcely equalled in Great Britain. Mr. Clark had a natural taste for the beauties of nature. He delighted to gaze and meditate on the works of God, as seen in the natural scenery of the earth. But now he could not keep his mind on these displays of divine power, wisdom and goodness around him. Other and more powerful emotions controlled his thoughts. More than a hundred times during the last twenty-four hours had the question arisen out of the depths of his heart, "Is my dear mother alive?" Alas! the affectionate son, whose longings to embrace his mother, and pour into her bosom the story of his wanderings and his conversion; and pour out his soul to God, and mingle his prayers with hers in thanksgiving and praise, never enjoyed such a happy meeting. His mother had been dead two years and yet he knew it not.

The schooner was safely moored at one of the docks in the harbor of Inverness, and Mr. Clark, having obtained his discharge, and bid the kind officers and crew a friendly farewell, proceeded up the city towards his native parish. A familiar name on the sign of a shop-keeper caught his eye, and he stepped within, and instantly recognized an old acquaintance. Mr. Clark in youth, as in old age, was of very light complexion, blue eyes, and light-colored hair, of moderate height, and light, slender make. The man who stood before the shop-keeper, was sun-burnt, swarthy, robust, and dressed in sailor trim. He could perceive some lineaments in his countenance which seemed familiar, but could not recollect when, or where, if ever, he had seen the person that now stood before him, while he leaned over the counter. Soon as Clark gave his name and parentage, both hands were seized with a friendly grasp, and a shower of welcomes was poured out in genuine Gælic; for though Mr. Mackenzie spoke English like a native, he never failed to resort to his Highland tongue, when moved by strong emotions.

Upon inquiry Mr. Clark for the first time realized he was an orphan. *His mother was dead!* The generous Highlander had the tact to understand that under the pressure of such intelligence, his guest would do best alone. Again he bade him welcome in plain English, and insisted his house should be his home while he remained in Inverness; at least he must not leave that night;—introduced him into a neat parlor, and, pleading special business for absence, left him to his own thoughts. This retirement exactly suited the feelings of Mr. Clark. He pondered over the parting scene with his father and mother; counted up nine years and some months since that time; recollected his mother was more than three-score and ten years old; that she was a true child of God, and died with a full hope of eternal life, and that the only trouble she felt was about the uncertain fate of her youngest son John. He learned also, from the Highlander, that his father ceased his intemperate habits soon after their parting, and appeared to have become a true penitent, and died in peace. A married sister who lived near Inverness had died in child-bed shortly after his mother.

With a chastened spirit of submission he fell on his knees, and with mingled feelings of thankfulness and grief, he found relief in committing himself and his surviving relatives to God. Before he left Scotland he heard of the untimely death of his brother Daniel in the island of Jamaica.

Next morning Mr. Clark left his hospitable host, and directed his course to his birth-place, the parish of Petty. He had learned that his only surviving sister was there, in comfortable circumstances, and managing the farm (held by a lease-hold) with the aid of a laboring man and his wife as domestics. He felt a desire to find out if his sister knew him, before he gave any intimations of relationship. He called at the house as a stranger, asked for a cup of water and the privilege to rest himself a short time, and entered into conversation on general topics, but could perceive no evidence of recognition. As if an entire stranger, he made inquiries about the country and its inhabitants, and finally drew her into conversation about the family, and asked many questions. The young woman appeared cheerful and communicative, and answered his questions truthfully and with frankness; told him of her father's death, without exposing his frailties; then of her mother, and a sister who had followed her mother. Then she mentioned her brother Daniel in the West Indies, who had been rich but lost his ships by being captured in the late war. The family history seemed closed, and no mention was made of any other brother, until with a careless air he made inquiry if these were all her immediate relations. His eyes being fixed on her countenance, he perceived a change. Her chin quivered slightly, her lips were compressed, and a tremor was in her voice as she named another brother, the youngest of the family, who went to sea before his father's death. But they had never heard from him, only that he had been pressed on board a war ship, and a vague rumor that he had been taken prisoner by the Spaniards; and she supposed him dead, but would give anything to know his fate.

John Clark had commanded his feelings through all the conversation, but he could stand it no longer. Every fibre of his heart gave way, and hardly conscious what he did, seized her hand, and exclaimed, while the tears gushed out like a fountain,—"I AM YOUR BROTHER JOHN."

We have heard him narrate this interview, when old and grey-headed; and he could not refrain from sobbing and weeping. Many persons are now living in Illinois and Missouri who have heard the same tale and seen the outpouring of fraternal affection, forty years after the event. The interview between the brother and sister, the only survivors of the family, was too sacred to be exposed to profane eyes. Though it failed not to work powerfully on his feelings, he would rehearse the tale of the interview on the request of his religious friends.

It was some hours before either party could obtain self-command to attend to the avocations of life. Each had a long story of trials and deliverances to tell. Clark found his sister devoutly pious. Her countenance bore the image of her mother at her age, and the mental and moral features held a close resemblance. As the evening approached they walked together towards the parish church. Around its moss-covered walls, was the parish cemetery, where slept the congregated dead of many generations. The sister led the way to a sacred spot she often visited. Here were a row of grassy hillocks, under an overspreading larch, with rough and plain monuments. There lay his father, mother, and sister, all buried since he left his native parish. Mr. Clark gazed mournfully on his mother's grave; on the head stone with dim eyes and quivering lips he read, "MARY CLARK." Taking his sister gently by the hand, he said, "*Let us pray here*," and as he knelt on the grave, holding the hand of his sister, he poured his heart out to the prayer-hearing God in streams of thankfulness and humble devotion. He praised the Lord for the gift of such a mother, so pious, devout and affectionate;—and for entire submission to the will of heaven in the loss sustained. He prayed for his sister, in language affectionate, kind and spiritual; *thanked God* that they had been spared to meet again in time; and that she was a child of grace, and was walking in the footsteps of her mother towards the heavenly Canaan.

Nor was the brother in a distant land forgotten, *if he was alive*, and that God would have mercy on him and turn his feet into the pathway of righteousness. Alas! That brother had been dead many months, as the letter that conveyed the mournful intelligence, testified, that reached his sister a few days after their first interview.

Mr. Clark had a gift of prayer quite uncommon. His language was simple, chaste, solemn and dignified, devoid of all cant, and peculiarly expressive. He seemed to hold converse with the Lord of heaven, as with a familiar friend. His prayers were singularly fervent and effectual, and remarkably adapted to the occasion and circumstances. He used no repetition of vain words, and despised all high sounding phrases and incongruous imagery, which some persons of inflated minds and heated imaginations employ in prayer.

Oppressive feelings were ever removed from the heart of Father Clark, in seasons of prayer. He arose from his knees with a smiling countenance, and wiped the tears that fell in streams from the eyes of his beloved sister, and cheered her heart by repeating the blessed promises of the gospel with which he was familiar.

Next day his sister called him to her room, and told him she had a solemn duty to perform, enjoined on her by their sainted mother, on her dying bed. She then presented him with a purse of gold and silver, of more than sixty dollars value. "This our mother made me sacredly promise to give you, should you ever return. It is your own;—the avails of your wages and prize money, the last you sent her, when we heard from you the last time. We managed by careful economy to do without it, and it is her legacy."

She then took from a drawer a set of silver spoons, and divers other family relics, all of which had been preserved for her lost son. The scene was most affecting, and it was more than an hour, and not until he had retired and held communion with God, he could obtain control over his feelings so as to reply:—

"My dear sister, the memory of our mother is exceedingly precious, and her maternal love and kindness overpowers me. I need not those articles to keep her in remembrance. Like my blessed Master, I have no home in this world, and I have really no use for these gifts. I feel that God has called me to preach the

Gospel, and in a few days I must leave you again, and return to London, and spend some time with that great and good man, Mr. Wesley, and study with his ministers, and then go back to America, and spend my days instructing the ignorant and preaching the gospel of Christ to the destitute. We must soon part, probably never to meet again on earth, but let us so live that we may be united with our dear mother in heaven."

After much urging, he consented to keep one spoon, and two or three other little articles, and told his sister to keep the rest, and to use the money for her comfort, or to relieve the poor and distressed. He had enough for present wants, and his trust for the future was in the same beneficent providence that covers the earth with herbage and is kind and bountiful to all his creatures.

Time fled away rapidly in their affectionate intercourse. Mr. Clark visited such of his old acquaintance as were living in the vicinity, amongst whom were several distant relatives. His habits of cheerfulness and his earnest religious conversation filled them with surprise. They did not quite relish so much spirituality and holy fervor. Some were eager for disputation on doctrinal points, and tenacious of their metaphysical speculations. They could repeat whole paragraphs from the larger and shorter catechism, and numerous texts of Scripture; and as Clark thought, with frequent misapplications. Not a few could talk eloquently about the "Solemn League and Covenant," and "David's psalms," while they condemned in the strongest language the versification of the pious Watts. But his story of his long and pungent conviction of sin, the views he entertained of the sinfulness of fallen, corrupt human nature, and the sensations of the new birth, and the joyful emotions of living in communion with God daily, were matters too abstruse and incomprehensible for their conceptions.

The most of persons with whom he conversed were very orthodox, according to the creed of their forefathers and the catechism in which they had been taught from childhood. All were church members and had been from infancy. They believed in original sin, effectual calling, divine decrees, fore-ordination, and final perseverance. They were quite clear in the doctrine of justification, and redemption in Christ; but Mr. Clark could not find many who could narrate what he called "an experience of grace;" his sister and a few others excepted.

The parting hour soon came, but the scene was too sacred to be exposed to vulgar gaze. On a pleasant morning, a modest looking man, about thirty years of age, drest in a sailor's garb, with a change of clothes, tied up in a parti-colored handkerchief, was seen walking pensively along the highway towards the city and port of Inverness. The Caledonian shop-keeper was visited, but no persuasion could induce the traveler to tarry. A coasting vessel lay at the wharf; and thither John Clark wended his way. He had visited the port a few days previous, engaged a berth as an ordinary seaman, and knew the day she was to sail for London. In a few hours, the wind being fair, they were moving down the channel of the Firth of Moray.

CHAPTER VI.

At Moorfield in London.—Returns to Georgia.—Received as a Preacher on Trial.—Richmond Circuit.—Testimonials.—Character as a Preacher.—Walked the Circuit.—Views on the Methodist Episcopal Government.—Views on Slavery.—Blameless Habits.—Thoughts on Marriage.—Love cured by Prayer.—Gradual change of Views.—Contemplates a New Field.—Quarterly Conference.—Conscientious Scruples.—Philanthropy to Negroes.—Withdraws from the Conference.—Parting Scene.

In a few days Mr. Clark found himself in London, and located at a cheap and retired boarding house in a pious Methodist family. He now sought acquaintance with several of the more intelligent class of Mr. Wesley's preachers, told them his trials and convictions of duty, and solicited advice. He was directed to the publications of Mr. Wesley, and also those of Rev. John Fletcher, of Madeley, and by reading and conversations with the venerable John Wesley, who treated him with great kindness, he obtained full and clear views of the doctrines they taught, the discipline they enforced, and their reasons for separate action from the Church of England.

We have no facts to narrate particulars of the extent of Mr. Clark's studies, nor how long he remained in the vicinity of Moorfields.

His interviews with the venerable founder of Methodism, then in the 85th year of his age, were frequent, and as he thought highly instructive. And though in a few years he found reasons to withdraw from the society he founded and the creed and discipline he adopted, he often referred to him in his preaching and private conversations as the "great and good Mr. Wesley;" and he would state his views on various points with accuracy and in kind and courteous language. He also became acquainted with the writings and peculiar views of the noted German Bengel, or, as his name was given in Latin, *Bengelius*, and imbibed some of his peculiar notions. Those especially relating to the millennium found in Bengel's exposition of the Book of Revelation, were often given by Father Clark. Bengel figured up the periods, and taught that the forty-two months, or twelve hundred and sixty days, expired in 1810, and the Millennium would commence in 1836. The Millennium, in the sense Father Clark understood it, was not the *personal*, but the more gracious and glorious reign of Christ on earth as Mediator and Saviour. On this topic he would dwell with a holy ecstacy, while his great modesty and humility led him to express himself as uttering the opinions of a man merely. He never attempted to make proselytes to speculations or opinions, but to Christ and entire submission to him.

We have no knowledge whether Mr. Clark commenced preaching in London, but as what was called "lay-preaching" was customary by persons not in "orders" in the church, or not officially authorized by dissenters, we are of opinion our friend did engage in this manner. We are equally deficient in the particulars of his return to America, but think it was in 1789; and to his late residence on Broad river in Georgia. No family received him with more tokens of Christian affection and joy than that of Colonel Wootten. His mind was now deeply impressed with the duty of devoting his life as an instrument of salvation to his fellow creatures. It is supposed he commenced preaching in company with the regular circuit preachers soon after his arrival in Georgia. In 1791, his name appears for the first time on the Conference Minutes of the Methodist Episcopal Church, when he was received on trial and placed on Richmond circuit[22]. This was in the region of Augusta. The Conference was held in February, and he went forth, as was ever afterward his custom, like his blessed Lord, with staff in hand, and on foot to perform the work whereunto he had been called. We find his name on the Conference Minutes from 1791 to 1796, passing through the regular grades of probationary service, until ordained as deacon by bishop Asbury in the winter of 1794[23].

The circuits on which he labored, in most instances, were new ones, and in that part of Georgia which lies above Augusta and between the Savannah and Oconee rivers.

TABULAR STATEMENT.

Year.	Circuit.	No. of White Members.	No. of Black Members.
1791	Richmond,	500	72
1792	Oconee,	220	21
1793	Bush River,	555	30
1794	Broad River,	435	68
1795	Union,	376	39

As a Methodist preacher, he was faithful in the ministry, and successful in the conversion of sinners. We have seen persons who were under his ministerial charge, and who spoke of him in strong terms, as an interesting and spiritually minded preacher. Of these we will name one, Mr. Thomas Hatton, who resided in 1834 in the upper part of Boone county, Mo., an old man, whom we visited for the purpose of learning the characteristics of the ministry of Father Clark in Georgia. Mr. Hatton was a class-leader and steward on the circuit of Mr. Clark in 1794. His house was one of the preaching stations, and he was with him at the quarterly conferences in the district, and spoke of him as a lively, spiritual preacher, greatly beloved by the people, and his labors as very successful. He *walked* the circuit, and could not be induced by his brethren to ride a horse. When asked for the reasons of his objections to traveling on horseback, he pleasantly remarked, "The Saviour walked on his preaching excursions in

Judea." There were other reasons assigned, and to his intimate friends he would say, "As long as my fellow creatures are made beasts of burden, I cannot feel easy on horseback." The fact is, he had never been accustomed to exercise on horseback, had no skill in managing one, and was distressingly fearful he should injure the horse, or the horse would harm him. No animal exceeds a horse in sagacity to find out the feelings and fears of his rider, and his behavior corresponds. No man felt more uncomfortable than Father Clark on horseback, and hence he preferred walking, until it became to him the least fatiguing mode of traveling.

We have given a sketch of his strong feelings and conscientious principles in favor of personal liberty when pressed on the man-of-war. These feelings and principles increased and became the more firmly established as he advanced in life. He never disguised his sentiments; and never announced them in any public form, without the clearest conviction of duty and in the way of doing good. Mr. Hatton stated that generally on his circuit he put up at houses where there were no slaves, while his intercourse and demeanor were such as to give no offense, or excite suspicions of improper designs.

The same views of equality and freedom, led him to investigate, prayerfully and scripturally, the ecclesiastical government and code of discipline instituted by Mr. Wesley, and introduced into the American conferences. Personally, and as a great reformer in the church of England, Father Clark had great veneration for John Wesley, but he was singularly scriptural and conscientious in all his religious views, and learned from the New Testament that a church was a local society, with all its members on terms of social equality; that church fellowship involves personal acquaintance; and that all discipline should begin and end in the local society or church, in which the members are in covenant relation. The more he considered the form of government of the Methodist Episcopal church, the more did he become conscientiously opposed to giving it the sanction that a minister and ruler necessarily implied. Yet he came to no hasty conclusions, made no denunciations of his brethren in authority, but continued calmly to investigate the subject and offer up prayer daily for divine illumination. He never set himself forward as a leader in schism, nor is there any evidence that he made the least attempt to produce disaffection among his brethren, or lead off a party, or even make a single proselyte.

At the same time, his sympathies were awakened and his humane feelings much afflicted with the treatment of slaves around him. That class of people were increasing, and their well-being less an object of concern to their masters, than the profits of their labor. Large numbers were imported annually into Charleston, by northern ships, and as the demand for laborers increased, many natives of Africa in the most abject condition were purchased and brought within his circuits. These were ignorant and stupid, and seemed almost beyond the reach of gospel ministrations. A single object was the aim of all his labors; to glorify the Lord by promoting the salvation of sinners of every nation, condition and color.

Being perfectly frank, open, undisguised and courteous in his intercourse with the planters, he had freedom of access to their slaves for purposes of religious instruction; a privilege he never abused, nor did he cause any one to doubt his sincerity.

Still the customs and usages of the planters were not congenial to the simplicity and humility of his nature, and it had been a matter of anxious inquiry, and prayer for divine direction, where the Lord would have him labor. He did not expect any other revelation from heaven than that contained in the Bible, yet he had such simple faith in the divine promises, and such unshaken confidence in God's directing providence, as to believe in and look for specific answers to prayer when in doubt and difficulty. He expected, and received impressions of mind, in answer to prayer, that to him were satisfactory, and we are not aware in a single instance in which he was misled by following these answers to prayer, as he called them.

It was at some period of his labors as a circuit preacher in Georgia, that his thoughts were directed towards marriage; and he became acquainted with a pious and sensible young woman, of excellent character and well brought up, towards whom he thought he felt such attachment as would justify a more intimate acquaintance. Her society was agreeable and pleasant, her conversation intelligent and serious. He made no direct proposals, but their intercourse had been such that she might naturally look for a more explicit explanation of his views. He found his heart was drawn out after this young woman, and her parents treated him with more than customary respect. She became the object of his thoughts by day, and her image flitted through his imagination while in dream-land at night. He discovered that when he ought to have been pondering over the topics of his next discourse, as he was slowly walking the pathway to his appointments, he was meditating plans of future happiness in the domestic relation. His spiritual intercourse with heaven was less frequent, his devotional feelings grew languid, and his sermons were dull and unimpressive. Spiritual joys were fled. It was now a crisis in his spiritual course. He durst not forsake the calling to which God had directed him, nor lessen his usefulness as a minister of Christ, by any earthly associations, or any schemes of domestic happiness. He had one antidote for all his troubles; one guide through every labyrinth of trial and duty; that was PRAYER, prolonged and repeated until he was effectually humbled, and entirely willing to know and do his duty. He could deny himself of any lawful gratification, take up the cross and follow Christ with resolute determination and untiring perseverance. He had acquired this power by growth in grace, and the knowledge of our Lord and Saviour Jesus Christ.

The answer he obtained in deep and lasting impressions of mind, was, never to marry and thereby entangle himself with the affairs of this world. The conflict was over; the victory was won, and he went on his way preaching, with renewed unction and great enlargement.

Though he had not mentioned marriage to the young woman, much less gained her affections and raised hopes, by solemn protestations and promises to be now blasted, he had that nice sense of honor; or shall we say Christian duty, to make her a final visit and avow his feelings, and the conclusion to which he had arrived on a point of duty to God and the church. He expressed the hope she would ever regard him with Christian friendship. His age at this period must have been about thirty-five years, and no one after ever heard him express a desire, or a regret concerning the connubial relation.

His anxieties about leaving the Methodist Episcopal church, and his feelings relative to slavery, were at a culminating point in 1795. His views of slaveholding were not discordant with the expressions of the church he served. This subject had been agitated in the Conferences for several years. In the minutes for 1784, we find this rule, in the forms of question and answer, and it remained in force during the whole period of Mr. Clark's connection with the Conference:

"Ques. 12. What shall we do with our friends that buy and sell slaves?

"Ans. If they buy with no other design than to hold them as slaves, and have been previously warned, they shall be expelled, and permitted to sell on no consideration."[24]

In answer to his oft repeated prayer for divine direction as to the field of his future labors, he received the impression, and it became a conviction of duty, that he must travel in a north-western direction. Tennessee and Kentucky were in that direction, and the Illinois country, and the Spanish province of Upper Louisiana far in the distance beyond; but he felt a calm confidence in Divine Providence, and that the specific field of usefulness would be pointed out in due season. All these questions were agitated and settled in his own judgment and conscience, before he made known his decision to his brethren.

The next Annual Conference would be in Charleston, January 1st, 1796, but it was not necessary for him to be present. His withdrawal could be tendered by some of the brethren. He attended the last Quarterly Conference in the district, where he gave notice of his intention of a withdrawal from the government and discipline of the Methodist Episcopal Church. This he had a right to do without any forfeiture or implication of his ministerial character. His brethren respected his feelings and scruples, and would give a fair representation of his case to the Annual Conference.

The schism caused by Rev. James O'Kelley, in Virginia, had commenced in 1792, and at one period threatened a formidable rupture in the Methodist connexion throughout the Southern States. Mr. O'Kelley was troubled about the appointing power of the bishop, and other features of ecclesiastical authority. He was a very popular preacher, and had the qualifications and desire for the leader of a party. He made both personal and official attacks on bishop Asbury, but the Conference sustained the Bishop by a large majority. Doubtless Mr. Clark accorded with the opinions of Mr. O'Kelley in his views of the undue authority conferred on the bishop by the constitution of the Society, but he had none of his spirit as a partizan, was in both theory and practice a peace-maker, and respected the views and feelings of his brethren, though he conscientiously differed from them. His views were deeper and covered far more ground than those of O'Kelley. All his notions of church government and discipline were drawn from the New Testament, and he regarded that as sole authority in the case.

There were also points of doctrine wherein he differed from his Methodist brethren. He could not reconcile the dogma of "falling from grace," with the entire dependence of the believer on the righteousness and grace of the Lord Jesus Christ; nor of sinless perfection with the universal fact of the moral infirmities and soul-humbling confessions of the best of Christians. And he preached repentance in a more evangelical form than many of his brethren, and always made the distinction plain between the awakened sinner, though under the most pungent convictions, and the truly penitent.

Such being his moral temper, and course of action, no unkind feelings took place when he announced his intentions, and sent to the Annual Conference the report of his circuit and announcement of his withdrawal.

His field of labor for most of the years he had been connected with the Conference, was on new circuits. Though not in name, he was in fact, the Conference missionary, and each year had extended the appointments in his circuit. At the Quarterly Conference to which we have alluded, the stewards brought in the collections for the preachers, and the deficiencies were made up. It had caused some uneasiness to the sensitive conscience of Father Clark that much the largest contributions came from the wealthy who were slaveholders, and he thought of the perquisites bestowed as the proceeds of the sweat and toils of servitude. He had heretofore received his share in the collections with many misgivings, and now as he was about to leave, he hesitated about taking such proceeds with him.

The amount of salary then allowed a circuit preacher, without family, was sixty-four dollars, and he had received but a small amount of it. The balance, about fifty dollars, was paid to him by the stewards, all in silver coin. He took the money, tied it in his handkerchief, and retired from the Conference room to a grove, his feelings agitated with the question of duty about receiving this money; and sought for direction in prayer, as he was wont to do in every perplexity. Obtaining relief, he returned to the Conference room, laid the money on the table, and calmly said, "Brethren, I cannot take it. You know my trials; the Conference may use it as the brethren please;" and again went out.

There was within the bounds of this district a case that called for relief. A society of blacks, of course slaves, had purchased a house and a few acres of land for a burying-ground. They had paid in part, but their last instalment of about seventy dollars would soon be due, and if not met, the property would be forfeited; and they applied to the Conference for aid. The case was called up during preacher Clark's absence, and one of the brethren suggested that the money returned by "brother Clark," still lying on the table, be applied to this charitable purpose. A smile of joy lighted up the features of the Conference, when, on the suggestion that there would be lacking some twenty dollars, brother R. arose and proposed to be one of ten to liquidate the debt. Mr. Clark having returned from his place of prayer, and being told by the president of the motion to dispose of his money, and how that disposition would suit his views, by relieving the black brethren, he replied: "Brethren, I could not conscientiously use the money myself, and I returned it to the Conference; it is theirs, to do as they please; but as they have kindly inquired about my feelings in the case, it meets my hearty approbation. It goes where it ought, to relieve those who have produced it."

In this last interview with a brother, who doubtless they pitied for his singular notions, there was not an unkind word said, nor a sour, unpleasant look seen. They understood he was about to leave that part of the country, and kindly inquired where he would direct his course.

"Like the good old patriarch, I am going to a country I never saw, and rejoice in the same Lord to direct my steps."

The business of the Conference being ended, they engaged in the parting exercises. The brother who presided gave a few words of parting advice, and called on brother Clark to lead in prayer, when with loud and tremulous voices, and the tears streaming down their cheeks, they sung the well-known hymn,

"Blest be the tie that binds
Our hearts in Christian love;
The fellowship of kindred minds
Is like to that above;" etc.25

while hand was clasped in hand, and arms thrown around each others necks, and loud shouts of praise ascended to their common Father. It was in this manner Father Clark parted with his brethren in Georgia, and took his leave of the Methodist Episcopal Church as an ecclesiastical institution.

It is nothing new or strange for a man to change his religion, or leave one sect and go over to another. And nothing is more natural when men are actuated by prejudices, or partizan feelings, than to turn all these passions against the party they have left. Not so did the good man whose history we are surveying. His religion was that of love; and his natural temper, mild, placable, and forbearing, was so much under the controlling influence of the love of God as to sanctify and give a heavenly tinge to his natural disposition.

Though he differed from his brethren, and in all honesty of intention thought their church government and some of their doctrines and practices unscriptural, he still loved them as Christians, and knew they were performing a great work in Georgia. Had he been denunciatory, overbearing, ambitious of ruling, obstinate, or petulant, their dislike of these offensive traits of character, might soon have degenerated into hatred of his person. We never knew a man more nice and discriminating in the line between his own rights and privileges, and those of his brethren. They might have felt emotions of pity and regret, for what they regarded as singular notions, and fancied these notions would hinder, if not destroy his usefulness. Still they loved him and gave him their good wishes.

His connexion was not formally dissolved until the Annual Conference met in January, when the following entry was made on the Minutes.

47

"Ques. 8. What preachers have withdrawn themselves this year from our order and connexion?

"Ans. William Ball and *John Clark.*"

CHAPTER VII.

Clark Journies towards Kentucky.—His Dress and Appearance.—Colloquy.—Hospitality of Mr. Wells.—Recognized by a former Convert.—Description of a "Big Meeting."—Persuaded to Stop and Preach.—Effects Produced.—Mr. Wells Converted.—A Revival.—Shouting.—Family Religion.—Departs.—The Wells Family turn Baptists.

It was early in the month of February, and in the year of our Lord, one thousand seven hundred and ninety-six, that a stranger was seen passing along the pathway that led down the range of low bluffs toward the Savannah river. He was on foot, with a small bundle of clothing tied in a handkerchief which hung over his shoulder, and was supported by a stout walking stick. His countenance was cheerful, as he tripped lightly along, without seeming to be wearied with the day's weary journey through the forest, with seldom a house on the public road. His dress was the ordinary garb of the country, coarse cotton and wool mixed, and of a greyish or light blue color. The outside garment was a hunting-shirt; an article then worn by all classes on the frontiers. This was a loose open frock that reached half-way down the thighs, with large sleeves, and the body open in front, unless fastened by a girdle or belt around the breast; the large cape fastened to the collar, and the edges fringed with strips of reddish cloth. The materials of all his garments were cotton with a mixture of wool, and spun and wove in the families where he had lived. On his head was a low-crowned felt hat, and his feet were shod with a kind of moccasins called "shoe-packs." These were made of thick leather, tanned by the farmers with oak bark in a trough, and dressed with the oil or fat of the raccoon, or opossum. The soles were fastened to the upper-leather by a leathern thong, called by backwoodsmen, a "whang."

"And is that strange-looking man a minister of the Gospel?"

"Yes; that is our excellent friend, Father Clark; called by all the religious people of that time, *Brother* Clark. Why do you ask?"

"Because he is dressed so singular and shabby."

"Why do you say '*shabby?*' I said no such thing. His garments are not ragged, for that is what you mean by *shabby*, if you understand the English language. His hunting-shirt, jacket,26 and trowsers were new, whole, and less soiled than yours will be in a single day when you run through the dusty streets, and playground at school; though he has traveled more than fifty miles."

"But he looked so strange and odd in such clothes, and he a minister of Jesus Christ? I never heard of a minister being dressed in such a singular manner."

"Ministers of the Gospel certainly ought not to be singular in their dress, lest the people think they desire to be noticed for their garments. I told you before, his dress 'was in the ordinary garb of the country.' Mr. Clark wore such garments as the men did to whom he preached, and therefore he appeared plain and equal with them. And his loose garments, especially in a warm climate, were far more comfortable than to be yoked up in a modern fashionable dress-coat, like the ministers in these days."

"But I should laugh so to see a minister in such a dress as Father Clark wore; it would look so funny."

"That would only prove you to be very foolish; or, to know very little. Suppose preachers of the Gospel should appear in our costly and fashionable church-houses, dressed just as Jesus Christ and the Apostles did in Judea? Would you be silly enough to laugh at them?"

"How did they dress?"

"Have you forgotten your lesson in the Biblical Antiquities, from the Sunday-School library, you read a few weeks since? There you learn about the dress worn in Judea."27

"Why don't our ministers dress as Jesus Christ did?"

"Because you would laugh at them. Nor would Father Clark have worn the same dress he did in Georgia and Illinois, had he been a pastor in Boston, New York, or Philadelphia. In such matters as were not religious and did not pertain to the service of God, but were earthly comforts, about which God has given no revelation, but left every one to his own reason and common sense, Father Clark, as did Paul, would have become 'all things to all men.'28 According to his notions of propriety, the dress he wore in Georgia was convenient and comfortable. The women who loved and respected him as a minister of Christ, made the cloth and cut out the garments, and gave them to him in the same form as they made for their husbands and sons; and he felt thankful and comfortable. Besides, he preferred to live plain, and economical, and by that means had money to give away to purchase the house and burying-ground for the poor Africans.

"But had he received a large salary as your ministers do, or possessed millions of property as the rich merchants, speculators, bankers, and railroad brokers now do, he would still have dressed very plain, and lived in such a manner as to have had the means of doing good amongst men. I very much doubt if even the force of custom would have induced him to appear before the people in a lugubrious garb of *black*, as clergymen do."

"What causes ministers to dress in *black* clothes?"

"Doubtless because they like to be fashionable, and be noticed a little for their distinctive dress. Some folks think black looks solemn, and therefore suited to the clerical profession. But, after all, a solemn, sour appearance is a species of clerical trick, which Father Clark never would perform. He was always pleasant and cheerful, and was the more useful for it."

"But still I do not see why our ministers should be so fond of *black clothes.*"

"We will answer that question, and then follow Father Clark. Black was introduced as a clerical garb, after the church became apostate, and was one color of the priestly garb. Probably nine-tenths of those who have worn it, both Catholics and Protestants, have been anything else than the true followers of Christ. An eccentric writer of a former period, in a satire on this fashion of an ungodly priesthood, gives this reason why they wore black as an official garb:— *"That they might the more exactly resemble their great master Beelzebub, whose garments are all very dingy."*

We left our old friend Clark, wending his way down the range of low hills that looked over the expansive bottom lands on the opposite side of the Savannah. Near the river was a house where lived a plain, rough frontier man, who kept the ferry. The house was a double cabin of hewn logs, and a space between the rooms about ten feet in width. The owner was sitting in this passage as Mr. Clark came to the stile, or steps by which the door-yard fence was passed. The sun was descending towards the western hills, and its face would soon be hidden by the range of forest-land along the river.

"Good evening, friend. Can I stay with you to-night?"

"I reckon you can, if you will get along with such fare as we have. Come in, stranger. Kitty, run and get the gentleman a chair; that's a good gal."

A blue-eyed little girl, apparently about ten years of age, brought from one of the rooms a plain, country-made chair, and Mr. Clark was soon seated. In the meantime the host eyed the stranger, as though he had seen him somewhere, but could not recollect.

"Sort'r pleasant weather, these days, stranger?"

"Yes: and we ought to be thankful to a merciful Providence for good weather, and all other good things in this life."

"Traveling far, stranger?"

"Some distance. I'm bound for *Kaintuck.*"

"Law me—'way to that country? And do you calkelate to walk all the way there?"

"Yes; I prefer walking to riding."

"Now, stranger, I begin to s'pect you are the preacher I he'rn tell of, who was at the big meetin' on 'Coon Creek, a year or two sin'. What mought your name be?"

"John Clark."

"That's the very thing. Here, old 'oman; Patsey, come here;" he called to his "better half," who was in the kitchen in the rear of the house, attending to her domestic concerns.

"What's wantin', old man? I'll be in soon."

Presently a decent looking female, apparently about forty, with a sunbonnet on her head, and dressed in a short gown and petticoat of the same stuff as her husband's garments—cotton and wool mixed—came in. No sooner did she cast her eyes on the preacher than she knew him, and broke out—

"Dear me, if this ain't Brother Clark, sure as I'm alive!" and she sprang forward and shook hands with him, with as much rude, but hearty simplicity, as if he had been her own brother; and bid him equally welcome.

This recognition of one who appeared as a stranger needs a little explanation.

More than two years before this period, Preacher Clark, and two other Methodist ministers, held a meeting for several days in a frontier settlement, some twelve or fifteen miles from the ferry, and Mrs. Patsey Wells was there. Mr. Wells had emigrated from Pittssylvania county, Virginia, to Georgia, about eight or nine years previous. He was not a professor of religion, but accustomed to hear the Baptists in his native State. His wife's father and mother were Baptists, and she had been in the habit of attending their meetings, and at times was under serious impressions. She thought she must wait the Lord's time, when, if she was to be converted, she would be; at least she understood the matter in this way from what she heard the preachers say. In the new region of Georgia, where they settled, there was no preaching, or preacher of any kind. Her husband got hold of a valuable tract of land lying along the Savannah river, on the south, or Georgia side, at a convenient crossing-place, where he established a ferry. In the course of a few years it became a thoroughfare on one of the principal roads leading from the settlements on the Upper Oconee and Broad river, across the upper part of South Carolina towards Virginia.

Mrs. Wells felt unhappy that her children were growing up without any religious instruction, and she could hear no one preach. But she had the care of a family to claim her attention, and withal became quite worldly in spirit, as their landed property rose in value, and the comforts of life increased. She was industrious, tidy, and kept on well after a worldly sort, but still felt at times unhappy, as if there was some great want unsupplied.

Mr. Wells was a good-natured, hospitable man, seldom got in debt, and then got out as soon as possible. He was reasonably industrious and with four stalwart sons, who were from twelve to eighteen years of age, he had opened a large farm and made some tobacco for the Charleston market. The reason he gave why he bought no negroes was, "he thought them more plague than profit," and he was determined his sons should learn to work, and get their living as he had done, by hard labor.

He really thought he was a good man, though he never served the Lord, nor thought of the high and responsible relation he sustained to his Creator and Redeemer, and made no provision for another world. True he loved a big dram, and the habit increased on him, but he only got tipsy, and behaved very foolish when he attended courts, elections, and horse-races; and mortified his wife Patsey by his silly behavior when he came home late at night. He was good-natured when drunk, boasted of his wife, children, and property, and never abused Patsey or the children; and would laugh, and tell jocular stories about himself, when he was sober.

His wife Patsey, as he called her when talking about her to others, heard of the Methodist meeting and felt very much like going. She had heard Methodist preachers in Virginia, but did not like their ways, and would have preferred to hear the Baptists; but none came into that settlement. One of her old Virginia female acquaintances lived at the place of the meeting, and she had intended for a long time to make her a visit; and now it would be economical in time and expense to gain two objects in one journey. So she left the "old man" and younger boys to tend ferry and keep house with the two little girls; and she, and her eldest son, went each on horseback to the meeting.

It was a powerful time on the frontiers; there was a shaking among the dry bones; and many a stout-hearted sinner fell as if slain before the Lord. There were three preachers present, each with gifts differing from those of his brethren. The first we shall describe, was considered as a sort of Boanerges among his brethren; at least so far as lungs and voice were concerned. And he used many "big words," quite beyond the comprehension of plain, illiterate people. Some supposed him to be a great preacher, and very learned, because they could not understand him. The second preacher was what the people called "a powerful exhorter." He could not work in the lead to any advantage, but he could follow a clear-headed preacher, and enforce the things said on the consciences of the people by persuasive language and apt illustrations with great effect. Mr. Clark after all did most of the real preaching, and every one on the ground heard him with fixed attention.

The meeting was held in the shade of the forest, where a "stand" had been prepared for the purpose. This was an elevated platform of split slabs, and a book board, breast high in front of the preacher, on which he might lean. Seats were made of the halves of small timbers, the ends of which were placed on logs, and covered over a space of ground large enough to accommodate several hundred hearers. In front of the stand was an open space, with low seats around, and called the altar, where the "mourners," or persons who were seriously impressed, were invited. At a late hour they separated and went to the houses of the people who lived within a convenient distance for refreshment and lodging. Prayer meetings were held at the houses at night, until late bed-time. Some families that came from a distance with wagons, brought provisions and encamped on the ground. Others, as did Mrs. Wells and her son, were accommodated by the hospitality of the people, and invitations were given publicly each day, if any strangers had arrived, they would find a welcome. This was not a regular camp-meeting, for those religious gatherings had not been instituted.

The husband of the woman whom Mrs. Wells came to visit, was a Methodist, and performed a principal part in getting up and sustaining this meeting. His wife had not joined society, but was a seeker, and gave evidence of conversion at an early stage of the proceedings. Mr. Clark took his meals and lodged with brother Lowe and family, where Mrs. Wells stopped, and it was under his preaching and exhortations that she became powerfully wrought upon, and was in great distress. In kind and sympathizing language Mr. Clark conversed with her freely. She had heard persons narrate their experience and conversion in the church meetings where her father and mother belonged, and had obtained some general knowledge of the gracious change all true Christians must experience before they are fit to join a church of Jesus Christ;—that a sinner must be under conviction, and have a "law-work," as the preachers called it, and obtain a "hope," as it was termed. But she knew very little about the nature of a real conversion, and the way of salvation through the righteousness of Jesus Christ. Her female friend told her she must pray earnestly and strive powerfully "to get religion;" and Mr. Clark showed her from the Scriptures the sinfulness and helplessness of fallen, corrupt human nature, and the infinite ability and gracious willingness of Jesus Christ to save her, and the mighty agency of the Holy Spirit in that work. He told her something of his own experience in trying to make himself righteous, instead of receiving Christ in all his fullness, and "who of God is made unto us wisdom, and righteousness, and sanctification, and redemption."[29]

This instruction had its due effect on her mind. Very soon she despaired of making herself better, and felt her dependence on the Lord to that degree, as to beg the preacher to pray to God to have mercy on her; while with an audible voice she cried out in agony, "Lord, have mercy on me, a miserable sinner." We have given some account already of the simplicity and effect of the prayers of Father Clark, but in this, as in other cases of prayer for sinners in distress, his whole heart seemed to go out in strains of the most moving supplications, as though he could take no denial;—as though the eternal salvation of the deathless spirit hung on the issue. Before he closed, Mrs. Wells, who lay prostrate across her chair, groaning and crying for mercy, as if wholly unconscious of what she said or did, sprang to her feet, clapped her hands in a joyous ecstacy, and at the top of her voice, in exultant tones exclaimed, "Glory to the Lord Jesus! Glory to the Lord Jesus!—he's pardoned my sins;—he's pardoned my sins!"—and with continuous shoutings and exclamations, until nature was exhausted, she sunk into the arms of Mrs. Lowe, who placed her in the chair. Here she sat, still rubbing her hands in ecstacy, and in a subdued voice, nearly powerless, still cried, "glory, glory."

"Well, I don't believe in such conversions as that," says a sentimental lady;—a church member;—though she spent the half of the preceding night over a specimen of the yellow-colored "light" literature that now fills all our highways and by-ways;—and sighing and sentimentalizing over an unreal and mawkish story of love and suicide.

"'Tis all fox-fire," declares a grave and reverend divine, whose intellect is as clear and as cool as an iceberg, and who has not enough of impulse to raise the slightest emotions in his soul.

"What a lamentable thing it is to have ignorant persons carried away with such enthusiastic notions," responds a metaphysical philosopher, who can map out the whole field of the human mind, and describe to the tenth part of a grain the degree of emotion one ought to have under all circumstances.

Those who weigh the impressions and emotions of gospel truth in one metaphysical scale; who cannot endure any excitement in others above their own passionless temperament;—who never had a muscle agitated nor a nerve affected by the unseen workings of the inner man, will have very orthodox notions about such impulsive feelings as Mrs. Wells manifested when she suddenly felt herself relieved from the burden of her sins, and enjoyed the gracious conviction of the power and mercy of Jesus Christ in her salvation.

It is a very queer kind of philosophy that admits persons to faint, fall, and even die under the pressure of some sudden and overwhelming calamity; or from ecstacy from hearing joyful news of an earthly kind, and yet accounts such paroxysms as Mrs. Wells had, "fox-fire," "enthusiasm," and the fruits of "ignorance." Mrs. Wells was a woman of strong emotions, easily excited, and never trained to disguise her feelings under a cold, conventional exterior. She behaved naturally, and under the circumstances quite decorously enough. No one was disturbed or interrupted by her shouts, but every unconverted sinner in the room became most deeply impressed, and the revival became general in the congregation. The meeting continued and the excitement kept up for more than a week; during which a large society was gathered, chiefly of those who professed to be converted, and Mrs. Wells joined. A new circuit was formed, and a preaching station fixed in the neighborhood of Wellsburgh; as some waggish traveler named the ferry farm.

It was not strange or singular that Mrs. Patsey Wells greeted Father Clark so joyfully, or that her husband, who had heard her describe the preacher at the meeting on Coon Creek should have guessed so readily. He not only spent the night with this hospitable family, but could not get away even had he desired, until he had made an appointment, and word was sent through the settlement for the people to gather for preaching.

In all frontier settlements in the south-western States, it makes very little difference in gathering a congregation, whether the preaching is on the week day or the Sabbath. All classes turned out in their ordinary working dress, for which they had a change of clean garments ready. They knew nothing and cared little to which Christian sect the strange preacher belonged; as all preached very much alike, and iterated the same common place truths of the Bible on such occasions. Men wholly worldly, and not very moral; who fingered bits of spotted pasteboard, drank whiskey, and attended horse-races and shooting matches, would turn out to hear a strange preacher, or go to a "big" meeting, as these large convocations were called; where several preachers of diverse gifts were expected.

The youngsters of the family were on their horses before the sun peered his bright face over the hills of Georgia, and rode throughout the settlements, and hallooed at every cabin to give the inmates notice that "mother's preacher" had come, and would preach at 'Squire Redman's that day. Of course every body understood the hour for meeting would be twelve o'clock. Though the people were scattered over the hills and along the vallies for many miles distant, the news spread, and by eleven o'clock men, women and children, two and three often on one horse, were approaching 'Squire Redman's plantation from every point of the compass. A full complement of dogs to every family were on foot, coursing along the margin of the woods near the pathway, smelling for game, and barking up hollow trees. The children of course, large and small, had to be taken, or the mothers could not go, and the dogs, accustomed to follow their masters and the horses would go, whether wanted or not. And should the young children cry and the dogs bark, both the preacher and hearers were used to such trifling annoyances, and never went into spasms, as we have seen a preacher, or a new comer from a particular section of country. In the vicinity of Mr. Redman's house, and near a large spring, was the "stand" for the circuit preacher, when the weather was favorable; and the dwelling house afforded shelter in stormy weather, for which the owner had provided rough moveable seats for the accommodation of his neighbors.

The preaching of Father Clark on this occasion was interesting, instructive, and impressive. Several of the hearers, besides Mrs. Wells and her son Jacob, had heard him at Coon Creek meeting. Wet eyes were seen, and sister Wells was in raptures; alternately praying with internal agony for her husband and children, and then smiling in ecstasy, as the preacher described, with an occasional incident or anecdote, the amazing love, power and grace of the Lord Jesus Christ to save the lost. Mr. Wells heard the text and the introduction with reverent attention; as the speaker advanced he was observed in an unusual position; his body was bent forward, his eyes fixed, and his mouth half open as though he would take in every word. Again, his posture was changed, his elbows rested on his knees, his hands supported his head, and a tremor seemed to agitate his whole frame. Those who sat near him saw the tears dropping fast to the ground, and it was evident he was unusually and powerfully affected by the sermon. This did not escape the notice of his wife, who was seated among the females on the opposite side of the stand, and every one could see she was exceedingly agitated. Others were affected, amongst whom were some rough looking, stout-hearted men, who never before discovered any agitation under preaching. Two of the youngsters of the Wells' family were among the anxious. Jacob, or Jake as he was familiarly called, who accompanied his mother to the great meeting on Coon Creek, had been serious at times since; while at other times he seemed to be more thoughtless, wayward and wicked than ever. He was there, said nothing; but held his head down.

Father Clark's sermon did not exceed an hour, but there was singing, praying, and conversation with persons in distress. 'Squire Redman, who was class-leader, gave a warm and feeling exhortation, prayed two or three times, and finally held a private conversation with our friend Wells, and pronounced him to be "powerfully convicted," and "not far from the kingdom of God."

We hope our fastidious, cold-hearted, philosophical readers will not get offended and throw the book aside because good Mrs. Wells had a paroxysm of shouting on this occasion. Those readers, whose emotions were never excited until every fibre of the heart seemed ready to give way for a husband and children, as she was, who she knew by her own sad experience were in the broad road that leads to the gates of eternal death, may retain their cold, calculating fire-side philosophy. But we shall permit this impulsive, warm-hearted woman to shout, and express her thankfulness to heaven in the strongest manner, and to her heart's content. A little too much heat and moisture are infinitely more fructifying in faith and holy living, than ice-bound cliffs and a region of perpetual frost. She had been praying for more than two years for her "old man and little ones," as she called them, and now she had evidence that the Lord was at work with them. Under these circumstances it would not do to stop the meeting, and the appointment was given out for that night at 'Squire Redman's house, and next day at the stand.

Father Clark, the Wells family, and several others tarried for dinner, and a good opportunity was presented to converse with Mr. Wells. Mrs. Wells and two or three other women turned into the kitchen with mother Redman, and by four o'clock, two or three tables were filled in succession by hungry guests, the men first served, the females next, and then the children. Bountiful were the supplies of meat, chickens, eggs, corn-dodgers, and sweet potatoes, with pickled beets, cucumbers, and divers other condiments; enough to supply a whole settlement, including the dogs.

It would have been the season of winter in a northern climate, but it was then the opening of spring, in the early part of February; the weather was pleasant and not disagreeably warm. After the first table was through, Mr. Clark gave our friend Wells a jog of the elbow, and they walked together into the forest to a retired place. Mrs. Wells saw the movement, tried to partake of the refreshment at the second table, but her appetite failed. She was too deeply affected to speak, and with another female who belonged to the same society, was seen moving pensively in another direction, towards the thick forest. We will not intrude. Her husband, whom, under all the rough exterior of unpolished nature, she truly loved, was in a most critical situation. She had conversed with him, kindly and affectionately, about his eternal interests, when he seemed in a mood to listen; she had told him incidents of her own experience; her agony of distress and the efficacy of Mr. Clark's prayers on her behalf. He had offered no objection to her joining society, though she knew he disliked the Methodists before she joined, and seldom attended the meetings since the circuit had been established. For the first time within the period of their acquaintance, he was anxious about his soul;—she knew it, felt it, and who will blame her if she and her female companion prayed for him audibly and fervently, while Father Clark had him on his knees in another direction, where no eye but the eye of God was upon them, and no other ear was listening.

Towards the setting sun, and as the people began to collect for the night meeting, Mr. Clark and his friend Wells were seen coming out of the woods, arm in arm, engaged in conversation. Mr. Wells seemed cheerful, if not happy, while the countenance of Mr. Clark was lighted up with a heavenly smile. From that day Samuel Wells was an altered man.

The meeting continued over the Sabbath, during which several others gave evidence of a change of heart and life, and when the newly appointed preacher from the Conference made his appearance at this remote station on the circuit, the following week, he found a revival in progress, and that his old acquaintance who had left the "connexion," had been at work in the Lord's harvest, and the Methodist society had sustained no damage by his independent labors.

Mr. Clark returned to the ferry with his friends, the Wells family, but there was enough of rejoicing and friendly conversation to occupy him that day. Besides, he must not think of departing on his journey before his clothes were in order, and everything ready; so mother Wells argued.

And there was another duty to perform which no itinerant, or faithful pastor, will neglect. Religious meditation, and especially prayer in the hearing of others, was a new business to Mr. Wells, and it required just such a man as Father Clark to encourage, instruct and lead him into the practice of household religion. Though his speech was somewhat incoherent, and a tremor shook his brawny limbs, in making the first attempt in presence of the preacher, his wife and children; he had decision enough to go forward, and soon acquired a gift that was profitable in the society and class-meetings. And now there was another serious difficulty. He had no Bible in his house; only a torn and shattered Testament, which his wife had read over and over, on the dreary Sabbaths she had passed with her family. Her husband had promised on two occasions, when he visited Charleston and sold his tobacco, to buy one. But on one journey he had made inquiry at several stores and found none; the other time "getting a little overtaken," as he called it, he had forgotten the business, though he did not fail to bring his wife a new calico dress, and several other luxuries she had not requested. The idea of Bible Societies, and special efforts to supply the destitute with the Word of God, had entered into the mind of no one. Nor could such books be found for sale in any of the interior settlements of the South or West.

Father Clark had a neat pocket Bible, which he obtained in London, and which was his daily companion. He was now in a strait betwixt the conflicting claims of duty. Generosity and sympathy spoke loudly to his heart to give this family his Bible. Conscience and reason seemed to say, "You cannot spare this book. How can a preacher do without a Bible?" After a season of prayer on the subject, faith turned the scale, "Leave the Bible, and trust in the Lord for another;" and so it was decided, and he never regretted it.

The parting scene was affecting. Mr. Wells and his wife both wept like children, and begged him not to forget them in his prayers, and if he ever came that way again to make their house his home. The whole family walked with him to the river bank, and Mr. Wells and his two eldest sons worked the ferry-boat over the river. As they turned into a slight bend in the river, they could see mother Wells still sitting on the bank, with her handkerchief to her eyes, deeply affected that she should see her preacher's face, and hear his voice no more; yet, devoutly thankful that the Lord had sent him that way as the instrument of salvation to her house.

The boat was tied to the shore, and the old man and his two sons walked with the preacher through the low bottom-land that lined the bank of the Savannah river, to the bluffs and up-lands of South Carolina. As they were about to part, the preacher kneeled down and prayed with them, and especially mentioned the young lads, that they might be like young Timothy, and serve the Lord from their youth. Mr. Clark was now seen slowly but cheerfully ascending the sloping hills, that led towards Greenville district, while in silence the father and sons returned to their home.

Leaving father Clark to pursue his journey towards the mountain range in the north-west, we will continue a while on the banks of the Savannah, to learn a little of the future history of the Wells family.

The rule of the Saviour, to judge of religious excitements and conversions, is, "By their *fruits* shall ye know them." Our metaphysical and philosophical friends, with the class of cold-blooded, grave divines, who measure the character of others by their own passionless natures; with the sentimental ladies who are dreadfully shocked at religious ebullitions, may be assured that the excitable Mrs. Wells, and her more sluggish husband, never "fell from grace," as our Methodist friends denominate the result of spurious conversions. It is true they left the Methodist society, and were baptized into the fellowship of a Baptist church, but this was in accordance with their original predilections and previous training.

During the period of Mr. Clark's sojourn in Georgia, Baptist churches and preachers were more numerous than Methodists. In the region south and east of Augusta, they were by far the most numerous class of Christians. In 1792, there were about fifty-seven Baptist churches, fifty-eight ordained preachers, twenty-five candidates, and about 2,400 communicants in Georgia. The Georgia Association had been constituted in 1784, and in 1792 included about twenty-five churches. The Hepzibah Association was organized in 1794, and the churches extended along the waters of the Ogeechee and Oconee rivers. The ministers who itinerated in upper settlements, on Oconee and Broad rivers, after Mr. Clark left the country, were Mr. John Cleveland, who crossed the Savannah river from South Carolina, D. Thornton, William Davis, Thomas Johnson, and Thomas Gilbert. Mr. Cleveland became acquainted with the Wells family by crossing their ferry, and they liked his style of preaching and that of his brethren, and being taught the way of the Lord more perfectly, with others, were baptized, and a church was raised up near their residence.

CHAPTER VIII.

Mountain Range.—Manners of an Itinerant.—Preaching in a Tavern-house.—
How to avoid Insults.—Hospitality.—Reaches Crab-Orchard.—Preachers in

Kentucky.—Baptists; "Regulars" and "Separatists."—Principles of Doctrine.—
School-Teaching.—Master O'Cafferty and His Qualities.

A range of high mountains is to be seen on the map, running in a south-western direction, and separating the State of Virginia from Kentucky; and then passing in a diagonal direction across Tennessee into Georgia. This range gives rise to the Sandy, Kentucky, and Cumberland rivers, on the north-western side, and the Clinch and Holston, the principal branches of the Tennessee river, on the south-eastern side. Through this range of mountains is a singular depression, called the "Cumberland Gap," through which the first emigrants from Virginia and North Carolina passed to Kentucky. And through this "Pass" runs the great highway that has been traveled for threescore years, from the south-eastern to the north-western States. The range of mountains is from thirty to fifty miles in width, and in the central part rises up in immense rocky ranges. The "Gap" is at the south-western corner of Virginia, and the south-eastern corner of Kentucky, where the extreme points of these States touch the northern boundary of Tennessee. Mountains are piled on mountains through this region. In the vicinity of the Gap is a ledge of black rocks near the summit, which extends thirty miles, with a perpendicular fall to the south-east, of two hundred feet. The Pine Mountain is on the border of Knox county, in Kentucky, and presents to the eye of the traveler a scene of sublimity and grandeur, not exceeded in mountain views. There is a view, the wildest and most romantic, where the Cumberland river passes through a gorge, dashing and foaming at a terrific rate. Here the limestone cliffs rise to the height of thirteen hundred feet.

Standing on a high precipice, from which the eye could range over a vast extent of country, on a clear and pleasant day in the month of March, a traveler was seen gazing on the scenery around him. Though his dress was soiled by a long journey, every feature and action were familiar to the observer. It is the Itinerant preacher, whom we left near the Savannah river a few weeks since; and he has ascended the mountain several hundred feet above the Gap, to feast his eyes on the stupendous works of Infinite wisdom and power. His mind expands with the mountain scenery; his imagination has carried him back to his native land; his adoring thoughts ascend to the Bestower of every good, for the protection he has enjoyed; hope burns bright in his eyes, for in the direction he is now gazing are spread out the fertile vales of Kentucky, to which he is bound.

He has traveled through Greenville District, in South Carolina, Buncombe County in North Carolina, and across East Tennessee. He has forded or swam the creeks and rivers on his route, but makes no complaint of fatigue, suffering, or danger. He had a small sum of money to pay his expenses, was never obtrusive, yet rarely did he fail of finding friends, and frequently religious families, who delighted to exercise their hospitality on so inoffensive a traveler. Unless the weather proved stormy, he traveled five days each week, and put up for Saturday and Sabbath in the bounds of some religious congregation, or in some destitute settlement where he could preach the Gospel.

Some ministers, even while young, are very annoying to families, by expecting personal attentions, seeming not to think how much they impose on hospitable families. Father Clark was particularly careful never to give the least trouble that he could avoid, and hence all who knew him were the more ready to receive him. He expected and desired no special attention as a minister; attended to his own personal affairs, and put no family to any inconvenience. He never assumed the ministerial character, put on no airs of dignity, and if he led the conversation, he could give it a religious turn without offence to any one; and he would leave the best impressions on the family without any apparent effort. Again and again, he was solicited to stay and preach with the people, with assurances of every aid he might need. On two or three occasions contributions were made privately and handed to him, where he spent a Sabbath and preached the Gospel, until it became painful to his feelings to receive such gratuities, as he needed nothing.

Two days before we found him on the mountain summit, he had tarried at a noted tavern at the foot of the long and steep mountain called Clinch. Here were men with pack-horses and peltry, on their way to the settlements in the old States. Explorers to the new countries of Tennessee and Kentucky, put up at this tavern. There was drinking, gaming, profane swearing, and all manner of vulgar and blackguard language. Mr. Clark supposed the time would pass very unpleasantly, but an elderly gentleman, who was on his way to Kentucky as an explorer, happened to fall into conversation, and found him to be a religious man, and on putting the question direct, the fact was acknowledged that he was a preacher. This gentleman conferred with two or three other persons of his acquaintance, and after consulting the landlord, proposed they should have religious worship before they retired. It met with general approbation. Every one present knew it was a free country, and he might stay or retire. Those in the heat of gaming, and half-sprung with whiskey, could have had a room for their favorite amusements, but cards were laid aside, and the landlord declared he never heard any say they regretted having spent an hour that night in hearing the stranger give a lecture. His preaching and exhortations were never in the form of denunciation, though pointed and plain, and well adapted to touch and arouse the slumbering consciences of sinners. He never failed to give evidence that his sympathies were awakened on their behalf; that he *felt* for guilty sinners, and desired to do them good.

He did not rail against drunkards, gamblers, and profane swearers, in his discourse, or manifest the least annoyance in conversation with any person; and yet all these vicious indulgences ceased, and every swearing reprobate seemed to put a double guard on his lips. All the company rested quietly, and arose cheerfully in the morning. The gentleman who had invited Mr. Clark to preach, approached the landlord privately, and proposed to pay the stranger's bill when he settled his own. "No, sir," said the landlord, "that gentleman has been a welcome guest in my family, for they have had comfortable rest, and if it had not been for him, we should have had drinking, swearing, and fighting through the night, to the annoyance of all quiet people."

When Mr. Clark called for his bill after breakfast, as he was about to depart on his journey, he received for answer, "Your bill, sir, is more than paid. It is not customary to charge preachers, though every one of that class who travels this road don't keep the house in as good order as you did last night. But you are welcome to the best I have, every time you pass this way."

Down the mountain range, towards Crab-Orchard, the country was thinly settled. Every eight or ten miles was a cluster of log-cabins, with stabling of the same materials, a rack to hitch horses at in front, and occasionally a rudely daubed sign on a post, that on close inspection might indicate that "*private entertainment*" could be had there. No public houses existed in that region, unless in a town or county seat, where lawyers and clients, judges and jurymen, could purchase intoxicating liquors to wash down their corn-bread and bacon on court days. Every farmer through the country, who lived on a great road, and had a supply of "corn and fodder" for horses, "and chicken fixin's," and "corn dodgers," with comfortable beds for travelers, kept "private entertainment." No one thought of getting a license and selling intoxicating drinks. The bottle or jug of whiskey was always set on the table at such houses of entertainment, with a bowl of sugar, and a pitcher of water fresh from the spring, and "help yourselves, strangers," was the courteous invitation. Whether the traveler drank more or less, or none at all, made not the least difference in his bill. Fifty cents for horse-keeping, supper, and lodging, was the uniform price for nearly half a century, at these country houses of entertainment throughout this valley. And if any one had charged Father Clark, a quarter or three bits30 was ample compensation.

It was early in April when our Itinerant reached the vicinity of Crab-Orchard, in Lincoln County. Hearing there was an appointment for preaching in the neighborhood, he went with the family with whom he had put up. The preacher was a plain frontier-looking man, dressed in the costume of the country; a hunting-shirt of dressed deer-skins, and trowsers of cotton and wool mixed, of very coarse texture, colored brown with the bark of a species of the white walnut tree.31 The house where the people assembled was a double log cabin, rough hewn, and when all had gathered, it contained about seventy-five or eighty persons. The name of the preacher was Jolliff; and he preached the Gospel to his neighbors and the people generally, as opportunity offered, without any thought about compensation in this life. He was a plain, unlearned preacher, and enforced such truth as he understood on the minds of his hearers. He had been, and perhaps was still a Methodist preacher of the local order, but he afterwards joined a class of Baptists called *Separates* in Kentucky.

Mr. Clark's dress we have already described, but it was in a style somewhat in advance of the good people in Kentucky, who lived many hundred miles distant from any market, and were compelled to live in a plain, rough way. Mr. Jolliff fell into conversation with the stranger, while the people were gathering, found out his business in the country, and insisted he should preach. Apologies and excuses are useless on such occasions for those ministers who keep their minds in habitual preparation to say something to the people on any sudden call, and Mr. Clark, though a modest man, who never put himself forward, consented. The people listened with attention, and spoke of him as "a right smart preacher." Some doubted what others affirmed, that he was a learned man, for he was so plain and simple in his language, and his illustrations were from things so common, that they understood every word.

Mr. Jolliff, who lived several miles from the place of meeting, was so much pleased with the discourse, that he persuaded Mr. Clark to attend the meeting in his neighborhood on the following Saturday and Sabbath, and to come to his house on Friday evening.

There were a number of preachers in Lincoln and the adjacent counties, all Baptists, though somewhat divided on certain points of doctrine, and not altogether friendly in ministerial intercourse. Each possessed his share of the imperfections of human character; each was more or less selfish; petty rivalries prevailed, and small differences were magnified, as each party looked at the other through the medium of prejudice. In a word, the pioneer preachers of Kentucky, were very much like the ministers of the Gospel in every age, nation, and country; no better, no worse; only a little more frank, and even blunt in their personal intercourse, and did not conceal their thoughts and emotions with the same ingenuity and tact as has been done in some places. Hence, if there were petty jealousies, rivalries, and surmisings, (all of which traits are wrong and unchristian every where,) they let their passions be seen, and the want of union and mutual coöperation was the natural result.

There were two principal divisions amongst Baptists in Kentucky, which were brought with them from Virginia and the Carolinas. The parties were called "*Regular*," and "*Separate*." These parties originated more than forty years before the period of our history.

The Regular Baptists in the Middle States originated from Wales; and in several instances, churches already organized came over as colonists. They settled mostly in New Jersey, Pennsylvania, and a corner of Delaware and Maryland, towards the close of the seventeenth, and during the eighteenth centuries, previous to the American revolution. At a later period, the descendants of these early colonists removed south, and formed the nucleus of churches in Virginia, and even in North and South Carolina. The doctrines they taught, as they interpreted the Scriptures, may be found in a little book commonly called the "Philadelphia Confession of Faith," because it was revised, adopted and published by the Philadelphia Baptist Association in 1742.32

All true Baptists take the word of God, the inspired writings, as their *sole rule* of faith and practice. There were some diversities among the Regular Baptists about certain doctrinal principles, as there were also among the Separates. These diversities in some localities prevented for a time cordial union, correspondence and coöperation, chiefly because they misunderstood each other in their modes of explanation. The differences in all the parties consisted in the way each party reasoned on abstruse points. Each put that construction on the language employed by the other that accorded with the peculiar technical meaning he attached to the same words.

The "Separate Baptists" originated in Virginia and the Carolinas from two leading ministers who, with their adherents, came from New England about

1754. The leaders were Shubael Stearns and Daniel Marshall. These men were Congregationalists, and belonged to a party that *separated* from the old Puritan Congregationalists of New England; being less Calvinistic in doctrine, and believing that such men as had grace, gifts, and a "call of God" to the ministry, ought to preach the Gospel if they had no collegiate education. This party were at first Pædobaptists; that is, they believed and practiced infant baptism on the faith and the covenant relation of the parents; but gradually they gave up this practice, and in the end most of the ministers and members of this party joined the Baptist churches.

Elder Stearns became a Baptist, and was ordained in Connecticut, but led by impressions of mind, with several relatives and brethren, removed south to Virginia, where Mr. Marshall joined him; and then to Guilford county, N. C., where they constituted a church. While in New England, these Separates had acquired a warm, pathetic style of preaching, and exhibited intense feelings. They had a sing-song tone, and their manner of preaching got hold of the hearts of the people and produced much preternatural excitement. Their hearers shed tears, cried out under great distress, and shouted in ecstacy on a revulsion of feelings. In a few months they had baptized about six hundred converts. Several warm-hearted, zealous preachers were raised up; one of the most gifted was James Read, who was very successful in Virginia.

At the first no distinctive names were attached to these parties, but the Separates from New England kept that name, which provoked the other party to call themselves "Regular Baptists." This name originated with Elder David Thomas, of Virginia, who possessed great influence, and was regarded by his brethren as a leader. Occasionally, and especially in seasons of revival, the ministers would coöperate, but the parties remained distinct, with the usual amount of shyness and non-intercourse, common in such divisions.

From the position we now occupy, it is easy to perceive that both parties had mistaken views, and employed inappropriate language to express gospel truth. The things for which they were the most tenacious were their opinions, or speculations; and many points were discussed in their discourses that were of no advantage to truth. On the disputed topics both parties "darkened council by words without knowledge."[33]

An extensive revival of religion in Virginia brought about a union between the Regular and Separate Baptists in 1787; a religious platform expressing their views in common was adopted, and the parties laid aside their distinctive names and took that of UNITED BAPTISTS.

The emigration of Baptists from Virginia to Kentucky commenced near the close of the revolutionary war, and the old lines of distinction were kept up there for about sixteen years longer. South of the Kentucky river, a majority of the churches were Separate Baptists, at the period of the visit of Father Clark.[34]

Mr. Clark attended the appointment on Saturday and Sabbath with Mr. Jolliff, and preached with his accustomed fervor and ability. The people who heard him were much interested, and urged him to stay amongst them. He found the settlements very deficient in schools; young men and women could not read, and very few books could be found. In many instances the teachers were incompetent, and in some instances too immoral to be trusted with the training of youth. He saw around him a wide field of usefulness. There were occasional revivals, but in general a religious dearth prevailed over the State. Revivals had existed to a greater extent in past years, but a general declension had followed, and a low standard of morals and religion existed. The Indian war on the north-western territory kept the country in agitation until after Wayne's victory in 1794, and the treaty of Greenville the following year. The tide of immigration was now setting strong from the Atlantic States to Kentucky, while a class of its population were on the move to the territory north-west of the Ohio, and even to the province of Upper Louisiana. Infidelity, combined with liberalism, came in like a flood and threatened to sweep away every vestige of Christianity.

Under these circumstances, and on the solicitation of many worthy citizens, Mr. Clark believed it to be his duty to teach school. This would not prevent him from preaching the gospel, for he would have Saturday and Sabbath in each week for that purpose. The people furnished him a cabin, such an one as he had occupied in Georgia, for a school house. In one particular he was singular. He drew up no article of agreement, made no conditions about the number of scholars, and exacted no pay; but left the whole arrangement about the terms of the school with the people who patronized him; only requesting them to furnish him with board and lodging at their houses, or log cabins, and such articles of clothing as he might need. Some thought him slightly deranged; others, from their habit of surmising evil of all strangers whose notions differed from theirs, fancied he had some sinister design.

The school opened, and about twenty stout lads and lasses were there the first day. Mr. Clark received each one with a pleasant, smiling countenance, gave them his hand in friendly greeting as they approached him, with a cheerful "good morning," and appeared at once to be on friendly terms. This conduct on the part of the schoolmaster, was, to them, a new feature in discipline. They had been accustomed to be greeted with a wand of hickory or hazel, (the genuine *birch* not being a growth of that region) and a stern, commanding voice. The predecessor of Mr. Clark was a rough looking Irishman, with a red face, and of violent passions. He was a disciple of Father Badin, the Roman Catholic missionary at Bardstown, and sent to Lincoln county—

"To rear the tender thought,

And teach the young idea

How to shoot"

in the direction of "Holy Mother Church." In this particular item his services were gratuitous; but he was unsuccessful in all he undertook, whether publicly or privately. He lacked every qualification for a successful emissary in the charitable designs of the good father. Mr. O'Cafferty made slow progress in retailing science and literature during the six months he engaged to teach school on Flat Creek, and such was the turmoil among his subjects, and so much whiskey did he punish weekly, that he found it economical to accept the compromise proposed by his employers and be off, on half pay for the last term.

CHAPTER IX.

Schoolmaster Equity in 1796.—New Customs introduced.—Mr. Birch Discarded.—Enrolment.—Books Used.—New ones Procured.—Astonishing Effects.—Colloquy with Uncle Jesse.—The New School-House.—A Christmas Frolic.—Shocking Affair by the Irish Master.—A Political Convention.— Young Democracy.—A Stump Speech.—New Customs.—A True Missionary.—Trouble about Money.—Mr. Clark leaves Kentucky.

The relation of the teacher and the pupils heretofore in most instances had been that of belligerents. It was his prerogative to rule and compel obedience, and hence "fighting," as the customary whippings were called, was the order of the day. Those pupils who were from fifteen to twenty years of age, thought themselves young men, and their proud spirits could be easily aroused to a state of rebellion. They descended from a hardy race, and had learned the tactics of warfare on the frontiers, where their fathers and mothers had to contend with untamed savages, and it would have been a dangerous business for even a brawny Irishman to flog such spirits into submission with a full supply of bone, sinew and muscle. Hence the boys from eight to fourteen, who had no brothers and cousins among these stout youngsters, had to bear their own share of flaggellation, and also the amount that in equity belonged to their older neighbors. The school house had remained vacant for six or eight months previous to Mr. Clark's entrance, and the youngsters gathered around him as we have narrated.

Instead of the expected order, in a surly voice, and corrupt dialect that was any thing else than the English language, Mr. Clark opened school by a friendly conversation with each scholar; beginning with the eldest. Divers questions were asked, in a pleasant, musical tone of voice, as "How far have you made progress in studies?" "What branches do you wish to learn?" etc. He addressed the young men as though they were gentlemen, and as if he was desirous of consulting their interests, and do the best to serve them. Instead of their usual boisterous manner of reply, their voices were subdued, and they felt what they never before realized, sentiments of reverence and respect to a schoolmaster.

In his examination of the older female pupils, there was some difficulty at first, to draw from them the answers he desired. They had heard him preach in the neighborhood, and were inspired with awe, and could scarcely speak above their breath. The little ones, boys and girls, he called to him, patted them on their heads, spoke encouragingly, and soon had their confidence and affection.

The next movement was to take down their names, ages, and the number of quarters, or terms, each had attended school. He told them frankly, he could not endure a school where mutiny and war were the order of the day; that his sole object in teaching, was to do them good and not harm, and he regarded it as the right and privilege of all who desired to learn, and improve their minds and acquire useful knowledge, not to be interrupted by the improper conduct of others; that he compelled no one to attend, and expected all who came to his school to conduct themselves in such a manner, as to make the school comfortable and creditable to all. He read a few plain, simple rules, and proposed them to the scholars for adoption, and even gave opportunity for objections to be made, or alterations proposed. This was another new feature in school-discipline and called forth expressions of astonishment and approbation from the older scholars. He was not anxious to enforce these rules on them, but to give every pupil time to consider their bearing, and suggested they could be postponed until next day, if all were not prepared to decide. The code appeared so reasonable and proper, that a large majority seemed anxious for its adoption at once, and every one present gave a hearty assent.

The next movement was to make inquiry about books; and here no small difficulty and inconvenience appeared. Each pupil had brought such an article for the reading lessons as first came to hand. One had a mutilated copy of Dilworth's "New Guide to the English Tongue;" another showed a volume of old sermons; a third had the "Romance of the Forest," an old novel, and a specimen of the "yellow covered literature" of a former age. A fourth, fifth, and sixth, could show Testaments or pieces of Bibles, with the binding in tatters, and the print dim, and paper brown, such as were gotten up for sale to merchants in that day. Some came without books or any aid to learn the art and mystery of spelling and reading. The Psalter that had descended from some Virginia families whose ancestors belonged to the Colonial English Church, was presented by three or four more. The marvellous story of "Valentine and Orson," answered for the whole stock of literature for a family of three children. What was now to be done? Mr. Clark neither scolded nor ridiculed his pupils for their deficiency in books. He knew they were not to blame, and he surmised their parents could not readily remedy the evil. There was not a book in the three little retail stores in Lincoln County, for sale, and it was between fifty and sixty miles to Lexington where purchases could be made. The world-renowned Noah Webster had commenced the great work of providing his young countrymen with the means of learning their mother tongue, about thirteen years previous. His *First Part of a Grammatical Institute of the English Language,* more popularly known as the "American Spelling-Book," was published for the first time in 1783, but it had scarcely found its way into the wilderness of Kentucky. Father Clark had obtained a copy in Charleston; he liked every thing American, and Webster's Spelling Book struck his fancy, above all others, from which he would like

"To teach the young idea how to shoot."

None had been seen in Lincoln County. Transylvania Seminary had been in operation in Lexington, ten or twelve years, where some of the higher branches of literature and science were taught, and many of the young men who became distinguished in law, politics, and medicine, in that commonwealth, received their education in that Seminary. After Mr. Clark had left the State in 1798, a Grammar School was opened in Lebanon, near the Royal Spring, in Fayette County, where the elements of Latin, Greek, and the sciences, were taught by Messrs. Jones and Worley.

The old books had to be used until Mr. Clark's new method of teaching became known, and one of the employers visited Lexington on business. He returned with two dozen of Webster's Spelling-Book, and more other school-books than ever before reached Lincoln County at one time. It was a real holiday for the boys and girls to look over these books.

The rude cuts, or coarse illustrations, as they would now be called, over the fables in the Spelling-Book, were examined and criticised, and the stories read, until they were "gotten by heart." There was the boy that stole apples, then on the tree, and the farmer throwing tufts of grass to bring him down, and threatening "to try what virtue there was in stones." Then came the country girl, with the pail of milk on her head, calculating the value when exchanged for eggs, these hatched into chickens, and the chickens sent to market at Christmas, and the profits invested in a new silk gown, in which she would eclipse all her female companions during the holidays. Inflated with vanity in her brilliant prospects, she acted out her feelings with a toss of the head, when down came her pail of milk, and with it all her imaginary happiness. And then there was the cat covered with meal, in the bottom of the meal-tub, while the young rats were about to enjoy themselves around the heap, until warned by an old and experienced rat, who "did not like that white heap yonder." "The bear and the two friends," furnished another fruitful source of mental speculation to the pupils of Mr. Clark in the recess of school; while the fable of the Farmer and Lawyer, and the amazing difference betwixt "your bull and my ox," caused bursts of laughter.

Thus the school went on, and the influence of the master in controlling the feelings, the minds and habits of the pupils in school, or even on the road-side, or at home, was overwhelming. This was effected by an unusual commixture of firmness and kindness, dignity and familiarity, never known before in a Kentucky school.

It was some weeks after the new books were introduced, that Mr. Jesse Bush came into the settlement from Old Virginia, to see the country and make a visit to his brother, one of the patrons of the school. Thomas and Susan Bush were two bright eyed pupils of Father Clark, and were discovered one evening by their uncle as he walked along the lane that led to the house, gathering strips of loose, dry bark from the fence rails for "lightwood." Such combustible articles in the fire-place were an excellent substitute for candles and lamps in new and frontier settlements. Uncle Jesse had taken quite a fancy to his nephew and niece. They had left the old dominion with their parents several years before this period, and had grown so much that their affectionate uncle would not have known them, had he met them any where else than at their parents' on his arrival. Susan was now eleven and Thomas thirteen years old, and delighted to play and romp with him, no less than he did with them.

It was in the month of October—the days had perceptibly grown shorter and the nights longer. A fire was pleasant and comfortable, and the lightwood threw up a cheerful blaze, while the industrious scholars were getting their lessons until interrupted by their uncle.

"Tommy, my boy, come here. You and I have not had a frolic to-day. You are at that new spelling-book every moment. What do you find in that book?"

Thomas ran to his accustomed place between the knees of uncle Jesse, and looking him in the face, and catching hold of his beard of a week's growth, responded:—

"I find a heap of things. Here are pretties.35 Jest look at that 'ere boy in the tree. He's stealing apples, and sez he won't come down."

"O, pshaw, Tom, that's all a story. You don't b'lieve a boy would get into an apple tree in the day time, when he know'd the old farmer would see him?"

"Well, I don't know, but the master said it's jest like bad boys, and he knows."

"Now, Tommy, tell me honestly, how do you like the master?"

"He's fust rate; and all the boys say so."

"How many times has he whipped you?"

"He duz no such thing. He says ef he can't get along without fighting, he'll jest quit."

"Has Sis' got a flogging yet?"

"No, *sir-ee*—Sis' and the Master are great friends."

"Does Joe Sikes come to school yet?"

"I recon he duz. Joe can't stay away, no how he can fix it."

"But Joe Sikes in old Virginia, was the hardest case in school. He had Mr. Birch hold of him regularly as the day came round."

"So he did here. Mr. O'Cafferty gave him some of the all-firedest thrashings I ever seed, and he only got worser."

"How in the world does Mr. Clark contrive to manage that fellow?"

"He jest talks it into him. And I he'rn Joe say he'd no heart to insult so good a man as the master."

"Now, Tom, tell me honestly which you'd rather do—stay at home, play with the dogs, and hunt coons at night, or go to that school?"

"I'd go to school as long as I liv'd ef I could have such a master as Mr. Clark."

"Well, Tom, I must give you up. Mr. Clark's bought you, that's certain. You're a gone coon for huntin."36

Calling up Susan, he said,

"Come, Sis', and tell uncle what you think of the master?"

"He's the best man in all Canetuck."

"But some of those big girls down the creek don't like him."

"Yes, they duz," responded Susan, whose whole soul had become enlisted in the mysteries of the new spelling book.

"Now, Susy, let me hear you read your lesson for to-morrow."

Susan had just commenced the table for "easy readings," and of course she had to proceed with great care. She took her station by her uncle, with the new copy of Webster in one hand, and pointing the fore-finger of the other to the word as her eyes passed along the line, she read slowly and distinctly, without missing three words:

"No man may put off the law of God;
My joy is in his law all the day.
I must not go in the way of sin.
Let me not go in the way of ill men."

"Well done, Susan;—you are right smart, and do your master much credit."

Time passed away;—the school increased, until the dirty old cabin was more than crowded. During the warm season, those who *studied* their lessons (and this was one of the new fashions introduced), could retire to the shade of the forest, and in groups of two, three and four, might have been seen by passers by, intently conning their lessons. But cold weather approached, the people became quite spirited in providing a new and better house for winter; and the whole settlement turned out with their axes and teams. Large trees were felled in the adjacent forest, and rough hewn on two sides to a suitable thickness. Clap boards, four feet long, were split from a straight grained oak for the roof; the ends of the logs were securely notched together and were placed one on top of another, as the four sides of the house were raised. In a few days a commodious house, about twenty feet square, and covered in, stood a few yards from the old log cabin. The spaces between the logs were soon "chinked and daubed;" that is, filled with small flat stones and chumps of wood, and mud plastered over the cracks both within and without.

For windows, a log was cut out from each side at a suitable height for the light to shine on the writing desks, which were slabs placed under the windows. The apertures were a foot wide and extended the length of the room, over which paper saturated with coon oil was placed as a substitute for glass. The chimney was built in the end opposite the door, and ran up outside of the wall. An aperture about ten feet wide was made through the logs for the fire-place. The chimney was built of rough stones from the neighboring quarry. And as quite an advancement in the style of frontier school houses at that period, planks, as the term was in Kentucky, or boards an inch and a quarter thick, cut at a saw-mill on a branch of Crab Orchard Creek, made a tight floor. It is doubtful if out of Lexington, and a half-dozen other towns, a school house existed in the country settlements with any other floor than the natural earth beaten hard, until this improvement was made both as an accommodation and a compliment to their teacher.

Mr. Clark had two or three young men from eighteen to twenty years of age, who had been under his tuition from the opening of the school, and who desired to qualify themselves for teachers. They were good tempered, affable, constant in their studies, and made good progress. The school now promised to have a greater number and variety of pupils than Mr. Clark could attend to and do justice to all. He proposed to these young men to assist him in the smaller classes, and by that means they would be qualified the sooner and the more thoroughly to teach and govern a school.

Time sped on, and Christmas, the *real* holiday amongst Southern people, was approaching. We are anxious to know how the tact and skill of Mr. Clark in governing rude, thoughtless, overgrown boys and precocious young men availed him on Christmas week; and as happened with other teachers in those days, whether he was "turned out" of the new school house by his mutinous subjects.

"To the time whereunto the memory of man runneth not,"—so reads the law phrase,—a custom had prevailed amongst the southern youngsters, that as Christmas approached, the authority over the school house was reversed; the young folks seized the reins of government. Judge Lynch held his court, and pronounced the authority from ancient traditions, that the pedagogue must resign all authority with the school house itself, until the holiday season was over, and make up the lost time at the close of his term.

The reversal of authority was usually effected the day before Christmas. This singular custom of turning out the master was brought from old England into the South by the cavalier branch of that nation in contradistinction from the puritans who settled New England. It can be traced back to the feudal age, and ranks among other frolics in which the common people were permitted and encouraged to indulge their passion for fun and riot, by both the priests and magistrates. A mere abdication of the office for the time being did not satisfy this ancient custom in all cases. If the mutinous party took the notion into their heads, and lawlessness and disorder were winked at by the parents, as in some settlements, the master must treat all the pupils to cherry bounce,37 whiskey sweetened with honey, peach brandy, or some other equally pernicious liquor. The same custom often prevailed at Easter.

The penalty of not complying with every exaction imposed by the rebellious scholars, was a severe ducking in the river. On some occasions serious personal injury has been inflicted. This feudal right had been claimed heretofore, and the master compelled to abdicate, and make up lost time in the school on Flat Creek. Mr. O'Cafferty had done more than his pupils exacted, for he had procured a supply of cherry bounce, whiskey and honey, and was so generous in its distribution, and set such an impressive example in favor of its qualities, that one half of his pupils were dreadfully sick, some had to be carried home to their parents, and the master required a wide path, and made tracts in a zigzag form, in reaching his lodging place. This hospitable trait in his character was no small item in the list of complaints, which induced his employers to get rid of him. Indeed, a large majority of the people in this settlement regard ancient custom more honored in the breach than the observance.

On the morning preceding Christmas, as Mr. Clark approached the new academy, he saw a number of the older scholars in a group, talking very earnestly; and he supposed mischief was brewing. He entered the house, arranged the benches and books, and gave the customary signal for all to come in, and take their places, preparatory to the morning's lesson. This consisted in reading a portion of the Old or New Testament, by each scholar who had advanced that far in scholastic attainments. All came to their places, when three of the company arose, and approached the master in a respectful attitude, as a committee on behalf of the scholars, who had that morning held a meeting on the due observation of the Christmas holidays.

We regret that at the period of which our history pertaineth, no newspaper was published in Lincoln county, and but one, the "*Kentucky Gazette*," in the State. Hence we can find no printed record of these important proceedings, and left for the benefit of posterity. Especially do we lament the inability to give, literally, the able and eloquent speech made before the schoolmaster by the youthful chairman, who spoke "without notes." As he is reported to have made quite a noise at the "bar" and on the "stump," after the era of newspapers, the loss of a verbatim copy of this maiden address is irreparable. The original copy in manuscript (if one was ever made) cannot now be found among the antiquarian documents of Lincoln county. Our readers would like to peruse it, but all we can give is the mere substance which tradition has preserved.

The speaker referred to the ancient and honorable custom of turning out the master at Christmas. He even expressed some doubts of the real value of such a usage, though it might be unfavorable to that manly independence that belonged to young Americans. He alluded to the unfortunate issue of Mr. O'Cafferty's liberality on a previous Christmas; indeed the last one the high minded young gentlemen of Flat Creek had observed (himself having been a sufferer on that memorable occasion;)—that the "old folks" at home disliked it;—that the young gentlemen who loved a frolic, really "had no heart," (these were the very words) to do any unpleasant thing to their present schoolmaster. Him they all respected and loved, and, therefore, the committee had been instructed to present a respectful petition, that the master would please to adjourn the school to the following Monday.

To which Mr. Clark responded to the committee in the hearing of the whole school in the following speech.

"MY DEAR FRIENDS AND PUPILS:—I thank you for your courteous and respectful treatment, and the address through your chairman on this occasion. I have labored to convince you that good order, kindness to each other, and a due regard to the wishes of your instructor are necessary to your own happiness. When we commenced our present relation as master and pupils, you adopted rules for your behavior, and you have enjoyed much happiness in obeying them. One of the most useful and important lessons for you to acquire and practice is that of self-government; for if you are not trained to govern yourselves, you will never be qualified to perform the duties of American citizens in this great and growing republic.

"It affords me pleasure to accord with your wishes, and give you a vacation during the Christmas holidays. I have been requested by preacher Jolliff and the people to attend a meeting with him in the settlement down Crab Orchard, and it will be quite convenient to dismiss the school this evening, until the first Monday in January. Now please take your books and go through the lessons of the morning."

Eyes shone bright, hearts beat joyfully, the books were opened, and all parties felt happy. The influence of Mr. Clark over his pupils received additional force from the manner in which the momentous question of observing the Christmas holidays was settled.

The religious meeting was held during four successive days and nights, about a dozen or fifteen miles from the school house, and attended by the people for several miles around. Amongst others, there were seen several of the students of Father Clark, who listened to his discourses with serious attention, and tradition testifies a number were converted.

But we must hasten forward with our story, for we have a long series of years yet to travel over, and many new and interesting scenes to portray.

The six months Mr. Clark at first proposed to teach the school on Flat Creek turned out to be a twelve month. A wonderful change had been produced in the settlement; indeed, we may say truthfully, an entire revolution had been made in public sentiment concerning schools and teachers. At the close of the year, he could have had one of the largest schools in the new and growing State of Kentucky, on any terms he had chosen to ask.

For more than two months, during the winter, his mind was solemnly impressed with the paramount duty to preach the gospel in a more destitute region. If ever there was a true missionary in modern times, Father Clark was that man, for he conferred not with flesh and blood, made no calculations of ease or a support, stopped not to see whether the churches, or other ministers were prepared to move forward according to the divine commission in preaching the gospel to every creature. He had imitated Paul the apostle in denying himself the comforts and happiness of the connubial relation, that no earthly tie might hinder him from going wherever Providence directed. He cast himself on that providence that so mysteriously had preserved him in perils by land and by sea, and engaged in the work of a Christian missionary with his whole soul.

When he left Georgia, his thoughts ran towards the Illinois country, where, as he had learned American families had gone from the south branch of the Potomac in Virginia, and the new settlements of Kentucky. During his residence in Lincoln county, he had seen several men who had visited the Illinois country, and even the "Far West," which was then the Spanish province of Upper Louisiana, west of the Mississippi river. There the gospel had never been preached; and yet, allured by the gift of uncultivated land for farms, and inspired by the daring enterprize of backwoods and frontier people, many families had crossed the Great River.38 The government of Spain was very despotic, but the commandants, who represented the crown of Spain in the province of Louisiana, were liberal, and encouraged Americans to migrate and settle there.

Of course with Father Clark, it was a subject of daily prayer that God would direct him to that field of labor HE desired him to occupy. He expected and received satisfactory impressions, or a full conviction of mind, after much prayer, examination of the field in Illinois and the Spanish country so far as he could obtain information, and watching the leadings of providence. The pathway of duty became plain, and to that country he must go, and see what the Lord would have him do there. We never knew a man who consulted his personal convenience less, and the entire will of God more. No man was more discriminating, looked at secondary causes with a steadier eye, and then trusted himself entirely to the Divine guidance.

As the last quarter of the school drew towards the close, there was evidently dissatisfaction and regret among the scholars. They had learned the intentions of the master, and they trembled at the prospect of losing a teacher who had treated them like reasonable creatures, and who led them in such pleasant paths by the strong cords of affection and respect. They really dreaded lest some illiterate whiskey drinking, brutal Irishman, like master O'Cafferty with his shelalah, should be engaged to tyrannize over them, and dry up every stream of true happiness in the school. But their fears were imaginary. Every parent and guardian would now have protested against such an imposition on the community.

Before the close of the last term under master Clark, it was whispered about that Joseph Helm would take charge of the school. Joseph was one of Mr. Clark's assistants, and showed much interest in the employment. He was a stout Kentuckian, six feet in his shoes, with a commanding appearance, and seriously disposed. The little ones had learned already to call him master Helm; and on the whole he was worthy of the mantle of master Clark.

The parting day came, and when about to dismiss the school for the last time, the affectionate master was so overpowered by his feelings as to be incapable of making his farewell address. He attempted to utter a few words, but his voice choked, tears fell like heavy raindrops, convulsive sobs heaved his breast, and he could only grasp their hands with nervous energy, as they passed him towards the door-way.

And now another trial came on. The women in the settlement had provided him with more articles of clothing than he could take with him, of their own homely making. Every house in the settlement had been open for him both as a visitor and a boarder, but the generous hearted men were resolved he should not depart empty handed.

Bank bills at that period were wholly unknown in Kentucky, silver coin was very scarce, and much of the business among the people was done by barter. The proclamation had been made for the employers to meet at the school house, and every one knew what was wanting. No one held back, and two or three who could not attend the meeting sent their perquisites by their neighbors. With no small sacrifice, about fifty dollars were collected by a sort of average, according to the number of scholars from each family, after excusing several families on account of inability. A committee of three gentlemen was appointed to wait on Mr. Clark, explain why no larger amount had been raised, and present the acknowledgments of the whole settlement for his very useful services, and their kind wishes for his welfare, and should he ever return, how rejoiced would they be to receive him again.

Mr. Clark had still a small sum left of his resources in Georgia, including the gratuitous offerings on the way from that country, and really *felt* that he had no need of money. When he heard of the meeting, he thought it had reference solely to the future school; but what was his surprise, and even distress, when the committee called on him that very evening, with their report, and the fifty dollars all in silver coin! He desired to treat them courteously; he respected and loved their hospitable and generous motives, but told them again and again that the people owed him nothing—that all he asked when he commenced the school was his board and clothing—that, in fact, he had no use for the money, and finally, that he might be robbed and murdered in the wilderness should he carry such an amount of wealth about him. This last objection struck the committee as having at least some practical sense in it, and after much parleying, he compromised the matter by consenting with great reluctance to receive a small gratuity as an expression of the friendship of the people.

"What a strange sort o' man that Master Clark is," said one committee-man to the others, as they were returning homeward after night-fall.

"Yes, he is sartin'ly mighty singular, not to take money for his labors when he arn'd it, and 'tis offered him."

"An't he a leetle sort o' crack'd?" asked another. "It looks like it," was the reply; "but, then a crack'd skull never could 'av' managed the youngsters as he did."

"Well, I reckon he'll suffer for that money yet, way in that Elenoy country, 'fore he'd find a chance to get more. I b'lieve a man ought'r get all the money he can honestly, 'specially when he's arn'd it, as Master Clark done."

"I'm mind he'll yet die a poor man, and it mought be he'd suffer a heap ef he lives long in that new country, and gets no money to pay 'xpenses."

"Well, I an't sorry we raised it, no how; for he'd orter been paid; for he's done the childer a mighty heap of good."

"And he's a good man, that's sartin'," replied the first speaker; "and ef John Clark don't get to the 'good country' he talks of when he preaches, I'm mighty fear'd nobody else will."

And John Clark was not forgotten in Kentucky for many a year, nor his singular ways, neither. There are a few old people still living, who attended school under his instruction, who, as they express it, "never seed the like on't." They do not believe, with all the "new fangled ways," and "heap o' larnin," and practical wisdom teachers now have, that they can come up with preacher Clark.

CHAPTER X.

Journey to Illinois.—Story of the Gilham family, captured by Indians.—Hard fare.—Mr. Gilham attempts to recover them.—Indian War.—Peace made.— The Family Redeemed.—Removes to Illinois with Mr. Clark.—Navigation of Western Rivers.—Story of Fort Massac.—Terrible sickness.—Settlement of New Design.—An ungodly race.—First Preacher in Illinois.—A Stranger in meeting.—First Baptisms.—Other Preachers.—First Church Formed.— Manners and customs of the French.—Indian War.—Stations or Forts Described.—PIONEER BOOKS projected.

And now we find the pioneer preacher trudging along the obscure pathway that guided him down the country in a western direction, towards the Green river district. He made appointments and preached in all the principal settlements as he journeyed, and was treated kindly and hospitably by all classes of people. It was in the Green river country he became acquainted with James Gilham, who was then preparing to remove his family and settle in the Illinois country, and wanted three or four able bodied men to accompany him, and work the boat down the Ohio and up the Mississippi. Mr. Clark had started from Lincoln County with the intention of passing through the wilderness on foot, but he had now a good opportunity of proceeding in a keel boat, or French pirogue, by water. They fitted out at the Red-banks, on the Ohio. While pursuing their journey of several hundred miles, Mr. Clark, in accordance with a long cherished wish, had a fine opportunity to learn much of Indian character and habits from this family. Mrs. Gilham and three children had been redeemed from a long and distressing captivity but two years before, and the story of her sufferings, privations, and wonderful preservation, as told to Mr. Clark, while sitting around their camp fire at night, deserves a place in our narrative.

Mr. James Gilham was a native of South Carolina, where he married his wife Ann, and commenced the battle of life as a frontier farmer. He removed his young family to Kentucky, and pitched his station in the western frontier settlements of that district. There he purchased a claim to a tract of land, and cleared a farm, cheered with the hopeful anticipations of a peaceful and happy life; but, like many others, he and his wife were doomed to disappointment. They had three sons and one daughter living, between the ages of four and twelve.

It was in the month of June, 1790, that he was ploughing in his corn field, some distance from his house, from which he was hidden by a skirt of timber, while his eldest son Isaac was clearing the hills from weeds with the hoe. At the same time several "braves" of the Kickapoo tribe of Indians, from the Illinois country, were lurking in the woods near the house, where Mrs. Gilliam, the two little boys, Samuel and Clement, and the daughter, were sheltered, wholly unsuspicious of such visitors. The Indians, finding the door open, rushed in; some seized the woman and gagged her, to prevent her giving the alarm; others seized the children, who could make no resistance. Mrs. Gilham was so alarmed that she lost her senses, and could not recollect any thing distinctly, until aroused by the voice of Samuel, "Mamma, we're all prisoners." This excited her feelings, and she looked around to find out whether the other children were all alive. Indians never walk abreast, as white people do. One leads off on the trail, and the others follow in single file, and are sometimes half a mile apart. One stout, bold warrior, went forward as a guide, and another kept many yards behind as a spy, watching cautiously to see if they were followed. They kept in the thick forest, out of the way of all the settlements, lest they should be discovered.

Mrs. Gilham and the children were in great distress. They were hurried forward by their savage masters, whose fierce looks and threatening gestures alarmed them exceedingly. The Indians had ripped open their beds, turned out the feathers, and converted the ticking into sacks, which they had filled with such articles of clothing as they could conveniently carry from the cabin, but were in too much haste to be off with their captives, to lay in provisions. They were used to periods of starvation, and could go three or four days without food, but the mother and her little ones suffered to an extent beyond the conception of our readers. But human nature can endure much in extreme cases. The feet of the children soon became sore and torn with briers; and the poor woman tore her clothes to obtain rags to wrap around their feet. The savages, as they thought, treated them kindly,—just as they would have done to their own children,—and Mrs. Gilham and the children had been familiar with the privations of frontier life, but they always had enough of plain, coarse food to eat; now they were starving. The Indians had with them a morsel of jerked venison, which they gave the children, but for themselves and the suffering mother there was not a particle of food to eat. One day they encamped in an obscure place, and sent out two of their best hunters, who crept stealthily through the thick brush and cane, and returned towards night with one poor raccoon. Mrs. Gilham afterwards told her friends that the sight of that half-starved 'coon was more gratification to her at that time than any amount of wealth could have afforded. She was in great distress lest her children should perish with hunger, or the Indians kill them. They dared not hunt near the settlements, lest they should be discovered.

The coon was dressed by singeing off the hair over a blaze of fire, and after throwing away the contents of the intestines, the animal was chopped in pieces and boiled in a kettle with the head, bones, skin and entrails, and made into a kind of soup. When done, and partially cooled, the children, mother, and Indians sat around the kettle, and with horn spoons, and sharpened sticks for forks, obtained a poor and scanty relief from starvation.

They approached the Ohio river with caution, lest white people might be passing in boats. They camped in the woods near the present site of Hawesville, and made three rafts of dry logs, with slender poles lashed across with thongs of elm bark, and placed them near the river, that they might push them in and cross over before they became soaked in water and heavy. The wily Indians were too cunning to cross by daylight lest they should be discovered, and Mrs. Gilham was exceedingly terrified at the danger of crossing by night. However they all got over safely.

The warriors considered it a great achievement to capture a white woman and three children in Kentucky, and elude all pursuit, and reach their own villages on Salt Creek, in the Illinois country, without being discovered. And they exercised all their cunning and sagacity to accomplish this daring feat.

When they reached the wilderness south-west of the Ohio river, they were in the Indian country, and proceeded slowly. They hunted with such success in the country between the Ohio and White river that they had plenty of provisions. They kept to the right of the white settlements near Vincennes, and along the valley of White river, and crossed the Wabash below Terre Haute, and proceeded through the present counties of Clark, Coles and Macon to their towns in Logan county.39

There they held a season of feasting and frolicing with their friends for their successful enterprize. And here we will leave Mrs. Gilham and her children, distributed as they were among different Indian families, and suffering all the hardships of Indian captives, until the war was over in 1795.

We now return to the father and son in Kentucky. They continued their labor in the cornfield until dinner time, when the horse was ungeared, and they returned to the house. There every thing was in confusion. The feathers from the beds were scattered over the yard, the mother and children were gone! The "signs" were too plain to leave any doubt on the mind of the husband and father of their fate! They were Indian captives, unless some were killed. The first natural impression was that in attempting to flee they were butchered by these monsters of the woods. Isaac began to cry and call loudly for his mother, until he was peremptorily told by his father to hold his tongue and make no noise, as some of the Indians might lie concealed, watching for him and his son. He knew the character and habits of these cunning sons of the forest, and stealthily examined in every direction for further signs. He soon fell on their trail, as they left the clearing and entered the woods, and saw in one or two places the tracks of his wife and little ones. He now felt encouraged, for he knew that Indians more generally kill persons on their first attack, and that when they take possession of women and children they take them to their towns that they may adopt them in the place of those they have lost, and train them up in Indian ways, and thus increase the number and strength of the tribe. White children who are trained by Indians make the smartest and often the most ferocious savages.

The country where Mr. Gilham resided was very thinly settled, and it was not until the next day he could raise a party strong enough to pursue them with any prospect of success. He and his neighbors followed the trail for some distance, but Indians when they expect pursuit are very cunning and skillful in concealing their tracks, and turning their pursuers in the wrong direction. When a large number are together, they divide into small parties, and make as many separate trails as they can. They will step with singular caution, so as to leave no marks, and they will wander in opposite directions and make their trails cross each other. When they come to a stream of water they will wade a long distance in the water, and frequently in a contrary direction to that of their journey, and unless their pursuers understand all their tricks, they will not fail in deceiving them. Mr. Gilham and his friends understood their strategy, but could not find their trail after they once lost it. It is probable they struck the Ohio river some distance from the crossing place of the Indians.

No one who has never experienced the same affliction, can fully realize the distress of poor Mr. Gilham, when, after a long search, he was obliged to yield to the advice of his neighbors, turn back, and leave his wife and children in savage hands. But hope did not desert him. He knew they must be alive, and he hoped the time was not far distant when he might hear of them. He sold his farm in Kentucky, put Isaac in the family and charge of a friend, fully determined to reclaim his lost family, or perish in the effort. He visited post Vincent (now Vincennes) and Kaskaskia, and enlisted the French traders, who held personal intercourse with the Indian tribes of the north-west, to make inquiries and redeem them if they could be found. He visited General St. Clair at Fort Washington, now Cincinnati, who was governor of the north-western territory, and who had just returned from the Illinois country. He learned that the Indians, stimulated by British agents and traders in the north, were meditating hostilities. Anthony Gamelin, an intelligent French trader, had been sent out by Major Hamtramck, with instructions from Gov. St. Clair, on an exploring mission to the Indians along the Wabash and Maumee, to learn their designs, and he had just returned with abundant evidence of their hostile intentions. General Harmar had commenced his unfortunate campaign, and the prospect was dark and discouraging. It was the intention of Mr. Gilham to penetrate the Indian country, and go from tribe to tribe until he found his lost family, but Governor St. Clair and all others acquainted with the state of things in the north-west dissuaded him from such a hopeless attempt. After a lapse of five years of doubt, trial, and disappointment, he learned from some French traders they were alive, and among the Kickapoos of Illinois. At the treaty of Greenville, the chiefs of the Indian tribes promised to give up all American captives, but a French trader had made arrangements for ransoming them; the goods having been furnished by an Irish trader at Cahokia, by the name of Atcheson. With two Frenchmen for interpreter and guides, Mr. Gilham visited the Indian towns on Salt Creek, and found his wife and children all alive, but the youngest, Clement, could not speak a word of English, and it was some time before he knew and would own his father, or could be persuaded to leave the Indian country, and he was left for a time among the savages.

Mr. Gilham had become enamored of the Illinois country, and after he had gathered his family together in Kentucky, resolved to remove them to the delightful prairies he had visited. As an honorable testimonial of the hardships and sufferings of her captivity, Mrs. Ann Gilham, in 1815, received from the national government, one hundred and sixty acres of choice land in the county of Madison, where they lived. Mr. Gilham died about 1812, like a Christian. His widow and most of the children professed religion, and some joined the Methodists and others the Baptists. A large number of the Gilham connection followed this pioneer to Illinois, where their descendants are yet living.

Mr. Clark and the Gilham family met with no difficulty on their voyage. They floated down the Ohio with the current, aided by the oars and setting poles, but to stem the strong current of the Mississippi, they used the cordelle and setting-poles, and occasionally crept along the shore by "bush-whacking."40

Mr. Clark made a capital hand on the boat, and cheerfully engaged in the labor and toil of the voyage. His experience in sea-faring business made him an acquisition to the company, and laid the foundation for friendship in this family and with all of the name until death parted them. Many of the Gilham connection became Methodists in Illinois, but Father Clark was the most welcome guest who entered their houses.

When night came on, they tied their boat to a tree at the shore, made a fire, and camped in the woods, where they provided their two meals for the day. They moved up the strong and turbid current of the Mississippi at the rate of twelve miles each day. Indians occasionally hailed them from the shore, but they were friendly, and only desired to barter venison for whiskey, tobacco, corn-meal, knives and trinkets.

When the company reached Kaskaskia, Mr. Gilham disposed of his boat to some French *voyageurs*, and made his first location in the American bottom, about twenty-five or thirty miles above the town. Both him and his family were hospitably received by the settlers, for they knew their trials and the history of their captivity. Mr. Clark soon found religious friends, and was ready to preach the gospel on these remote frontiers.

The Indians of the north-west had been so severely chastised by "Mad Anthony," (as the soldiers call General Wayne,) that they were glad to make peace; and now, after many years of distress, and the massacre of many families in the Illinois country, the people had opportunity to cultivate their little farms, and provide the necessaries to enable them to live comfortably. The people then travelled from the older settlements to this frontier country, and even caravans of moving families went down the Ohio in flat boats, with their horses, cattle, provisions, and clothing, to a place called *Massac* by the French, from whence they followed a trail through the wilderness, with their wagons or pack horses, to Kaskaskia, and to the settlement of New Design, and the American bottom, thirty miles further. Massac was a contracted form of speech for *Massacre*, in the French mode of abbreviating proper names. It is on the Ohio river, near where the town of Metropolis is now situated, which is the seat of justice for Massac County. Its name is a memento of a fearful calamity in the early part of the last century. The French established a trading post and a missionary station on the right bank of the Ohio, then called *Ouabache*. The southern Indians, then hostile to these Europeans, laid a stratagem to obtain possession of the fort. A number of them appeared in the day-time on the sand-bar of the opposite side of the river, each covered with the skin of a bear, and walking on all fours. They had disguised themselves so completely, and played pantomime so successfully with each other, that the French people did not doubt they were really wild bears from the forest who came there to drink. A party crossed the river in pursuit of them, while the rest left the fort and stood on the bank to see the sport. They did not discover the deception until they found themselves cut off from returning within the fort. They were soon massacred by the tomahawk and scalping knife of the savages. The French built another fort on the same spot, afterwards, and called it Massacre, or, as they taught the American pioneers to call it, MASSAC.

Early in the same season that Mr. Clark came with the Gilham family, a colony of one hundred and twenty-six emigrants from the south branch of the Potomac in Virginia, set out for Illinois. At Redstone, on the Monongahela, (now Brownsville,) they fitted out several flat boats, on which, with their horses and wagons, they floated down the current to Pittsburgh, and thence down the Ohio to Massac, where they landed and went across the country to the settlement of New Design. That season, and especially after they left the Ohio, was unusually rainy and hot. The streams overflowed their banks, and covered the alluvial, or bottom lands on their borders; and the low ground in the woods and prairies were covered with water. They were twenty-one days traveling through this wilderness, the distance of about one hundred miles, and much of it through dreary forests. The old settlers had been so long harassed with Indian warfare, that farming business had been neglected, their cattle were few in number, and bread corn was scarce. Their cabins usually contained each a single room for all domestic purposes; and though hospitality to strangers is a universal trait in frontier character, it was entirely beyond the ability of the inhabitants to provide accommodations for these 'new comers,' who arrived in a deplorably famishing and sickly condition. They did all they could; a single cabin frequently contained four or five families. Their rifles could provide venison from the woods, but the weather that followed the severe rains in midsummer was so unusually hot and sultry, that their fresh meat spoiled before they could pack it from the hunting grounds; and they were destitute of salt to preserve and season it. Medical aid could be procured only from a great distance, and that very seldom. Under such circumstances, no one need be surprised that of the colony, who left Virginia in the Spring, only one-half of their number were alive in autumn. A ridge in the western part of the settlement, adjacent to the bluffs, was covered with the newly formed graves. They were swept off by a putrid fever, unusually malignant, and which, in some instances, did its work in a few hours. The old settlers were as healthy as usual. No disease like this ever appeared in the country before or since. Mr. Clark had good health, and found work enough among these suffering families in nursing, instructing, and praying with the sick, and consoling the dying. The settlement of New Design had been commenced by American families about a dozen years previous. Its situation was on the elevated plateau, about thirty miles north of the town of Kaskaskia, and from ten to twelve miles from the Mississippi, and from three to six miles east of the American bottom and contiguous bluffs. Along the wide alluvial tract, or bottom, there were American families settled at intervals from Prairie du Rocher to the vicinity of Cahokia. The character of the American families was various. Some were religious people, both Baptists and Methodists; some were moral, and respected the Sabbath; others were infidels, or at least skeptical of all revealed truth. They paid no regard to religious meetings, and permitted their children to grow up without any moral restraint. They were fond of frolics, dances, horse-racing, card playing, and other vices, in which they were joined by many of the French population from the villages. They drank *tafia*,41 and when fruit became plenty, peach brandy was made, and rye whiskey obtained from the Monongahela country.

There has been a very marked difference between these two classes of pioneers, down to the third and fourth generation. But a very few of the descendants of the immoral and irreligious class are to be found amongst the present generation of the religious, moral, industrious and enterprising class. They followed the footsteps of their fathers, and have wasted away. Even the names of a number of these pioneer families have been blotted out, while the children's children, of the virtuous class, are numerous and respected.

There were several families in the very commencement of these settlements, before a preacher of the Gospel brought the glad tidings here, or a single person had made a profession of religion, that held meetings on the Sabbath, read portions of the Scriptures, or a sermon, and sang hymns, and thus set a good example to the others. They and their descendants have been favored of the Lord.

The first preacher who visited the Illinois country, was James Smith, from Lincoln County, Ky. He was a "Separate Baptist," and came on business, in 1787, but preached to the people repeatedly, and many of those who had kept up the meetings just noticed, professed conversion under his preaching. Of these the Hon. Shadrach Bond, Captain Joseph Ogle, James Lemen, Sen., his son-in-law, were conspicuous persons. He made another visit to the country in 1790, after the Indians had become troublesome, and preached with similar effect. While riding to the meeting place, on a week day, in company with another man, and a Mrs. Huff, they were fired at by a party of Kickapoos in ambuscade, near the present site of Waterloo, in Monroe county. Mrs. Huff was killed and scalped. The other man was wounded, but escaped with his horse, and Mr. Smith taken prisoner. The Indians took him through the prairies to their town on the Wabash, but he was afterwards ransomed through the agency of a French trader. After the visits and preaching of Mr. Smith, there were persons who could pray in these social meetings, and when it was safe to live out of forts, they met at each others houses, and Judge Bond, James Piggott, James Lemen, and some others, conducted the worship.

It was in January, 1794, while Judge Bond was officiating in this informal manner on the Sabbath, that a stranger came into the log cabin, where the people had assembled. He was a large, portly man, with dark hair, a florid complexion, and regular features. His dress was in advance of the deer-skin hunting shirts and Indian moccasins of the settlers; his countenance was grave and dignified, and his aspect so serious, that the reader was impressed with the thought that he was a professor of religion; perhaps a preacher, and an invitation was given him "to close the exercises, if he was a praying man." The stranger kneeled, and made an impressive, fluent, and solemn prayer.

There was a man in the congregation, of small talents, and rather narrow views, who, from his national origin, bore the *soubriquet* of Dutch Pete among the people; or Peter Smith, as his name appears in the land documents. Pete was a zealous Methodist, and when his own preachers prayed, he felt moved by the Spirit to utter *Amen*, at the close of every sentence. While the people were on their knees, or with their heads bowed low on their seats, Pete manifested much uneasiness at the prayer of the stranger. He fidgetted one way and then another, uttered a low, but audible groan, and to those near him seemed to be in trouble. The very impressive and earnest prayer of the speaker excited his feelings beyond suppression. He might not be a Methodist; but Pete could hold in no longer, and bawled out, at the top of his voice, "*Amen, at a wenture!*"

The stranger proved to be Rev. Josiah Dodge, from Nelson county, Kentucky. He had been to St. Genevieve on a visit to his brother, Doctor Israel Dodge, and hearing of these religious people being entirely destitute of ministerial instruction, he had arrived opportunely to preach to them.

Mr. Dodge spent some time in the settlement, preaching daily, and visiting from house to house, and in February, the ice was cut in Fountain Creek; all the people for many miles around were present, and there he baptized James Lemen, Sen., and Catharine his wife; John Gibbons and Isaac Enochs, who were the first persons ever baptized in this territory.42

During the next two years, the people remained without preachers; but both Baptists and Methodists, without organized societies, united in holding prayer-meetings, in which, as formerly, the Scriptures and sermon books were read, prayers offered and hymns sung in praise to God.

The year previous to the visit of Mr. Dodge, Rev. Joseph Lillard made an excursion to the Illinois country. He was a Methodist, and in 1790-'91, was in the traveling connection in Kentucky, but he withdrew from that connection from objections to the government and discipline, and like Mr. Clark occupied an independent position. He preached to the people and organized a class, the first ever formed in this country, and appointed Captain Joseph Ogle the leader. Mr. Lillard was esteemed by all who knew him, as a pious and exemplary man; but while in Illinois he became temporarily deranged, made his escape from his friends and outran them, and followed the trail towards Kaskaskia. On the route he came across the body of a man by the name of Sipp, whom the Indians had killed and scalped. While gazing at this horrid sight, he became calm, his reason and consciousness were restored, and he returned to his friends at New Design, and made report of the discovery. The people made up a party who visited the place and buried the unfortunate man.

From time to time, Baptists came into these settlements, so that by May, 1796, there were ten or a dozen men and women in the country who had been members of churches in Virginia or Kentucky, from whence they came. Among these was Joseph Chance, who was an exhorter, and also a *lay-elder*, from Shelby county, Kentucky. This office, now unknown in Baptist churches, was regarded in Virginia and afterwards for a time in Kentucky, as an appendage to the pastoral office. Lay-elders had no authority in government and discipline, as in a Presbyterian church, but aided the pastor in conducting religious meetings by exhortation and prayer, visiting the sick, instructing the ignorant, and confirming the wavering. Mr. Chance afterwards became an ordained minister. He did not possess great talents as a preacher, but was faithful in the exercise of the gifts bestowed on him, loved religious meetings, devoted much time to preaching and visiting destitute settlements, and died while on a preaching tour in 1840, aged seventy-five years.

The Baptists in Illinois did not appear to know they could have formed themselves into a church, and chose such gifts as they had amongst them as leaders; and kept up the worship of God without the authority of an ordained minister. In the spring of 1796, Rev. David Badgley, of Hardy county, Va., made a visit to the Illinois country. He arrived in the settlement of New Design on the 4th of May, and preached night and day until the 30th, during which time he baptized fifteen persons on a profession of faith in Christ, and with the aid of Mr. Chance organized the first Baptist church ever formed in this country, of twenty-eight members. He returned to Virginia the same season, and the next spring (1797,) came back with his family and several others to settle this new country.

At that period the white population of the Illinois country, numbered about 2,700, of which about two-thirds were of French descent, spoke that language, and followed the customs of the Canadians, from whence most of their forefathers originated. They were a contented race of people, patient under hardships, without ambition, and ignorant of the prolific resources of the country. They never troubled themselves with political matters, engaged in no schemes of aggrandizement, and showed no inclination for political domination. They were a frank, open-hearted, joyous people, and careless about the acquisition of property. Their houses were small, built of logs set upright, like palisades, with the spaces filled in, plastered, and neatly white-washed inside and out. They cultivated fruits and flowers, and in this respect showed taste and refinement beyond the Americans. In religion they were nominally Roman Catholics; in the morning of the Sabbath they attended mass, and in the afternoon visited, played the violin, danced, or engaged in other recreations and ruder sports out of doors.

Another pioneer who was an exhorter in the Methodist connection, and came to the country in 1796, was the late Rev. Hosea Riggs, who at first settled in the American bottom. Mr. Riggs was born in Western Pennsylvania in 1760, became a soldier in the revolutionary war; and when twenty-two years of age, he enlisted in the army of Jesus Christ and joined the Methodist Episcopal church, became an exhorter, and proved himself a diligent and faithful soldier of the cross. When he arrived in the Illinois country with his family he found Capt. Joseph Ogle and family, Peter Casterline and family, and William Murray from Ireland, the remains of the class formed by Mr. Lillard. These he re-organized into a class at Captain Ogle's house, and at a subsequent period formed another class of immigrant Methodists, in Goshen settlement. This was in Madison county, between Edwardsville and the American bottom. Mr. Riggs, though then only a licensed exhorter, attended these Methodist classes, and made appointments for meetings for six years. He attended the "Western Conference" in Kentucky, 1803, raised a Macedonian cry, and the Conference sent Rev. Benjamin Young as a missionary, who was the first preacher of the Methodist Episcopal church who traveled the circuit in Illinois. Mr. Riggs was tenacious for the Methodist government and discipline, and hence did not so readily coöperate with Father Clark. He was a good man, a faithful preacher, lived a Christian life, and died a Christian death, in St. Clair county, in 1841, at the age of eighty-one years.

We have now brought up the religious history of Illinois to the period of the arrival of Mr. Clark. But to give our young readers a fuller picture of frontier life, and of the people with whom he lived and labored, and their deprivations, we must again look back on their condition for a few years past.

From 1786, to 1795, the American settlements in the Illinois country, as was the case throughout the north-western territory, were harrassed by hostile Indians. A part of the time the families were compelled to live in forts, or as they were called, "stations."

A square was marked out, in proportion to the number of families. On two sides log cabins were erected in rows, with the roof sloping to the inner side of the enclosure. Block houses were put up at the corners, and so constructed that in the upper part which jutted over the lower story, the guard could watch the approach of the enemy and attack them successfully. The spaces not occupied by cabins were filled up with palisades. Strong doors made of thick slabs, or split timbers protected the places of ingress and egress. These stations were a sufficient protection against the small marauding parties, that came stealthily into the settlements. When no signs of hostile Indians were seen for some months, the people, tired of living in these stations, would remove to their cabins and attempt to raise a crop, when the first alarm would be by some family being massacred, or individual killed, in attempting to pass from one settlement to another. We could give many thrilling instances of savage barbarity, but our space is limited. They shall all be told, if we are successful in getting out our projected series of PIONEER BOOKS.

While the women and children were compelled to stay in forts, the men cultivated a field in common within sight of the station, and one party with their trusty rifles scouted around as a guard, while another party plowed and planted corn. No schools nor regular religious meetings could be held during these Indian invasions.

When they ventured out of the forts, and resided on their farms, in the absence of the men, pious mothers barricaded the door lest Indians might come on them suddenly, and gathered the little children around the huge fire place, for the light that shone down the large chimneys, and taught them the rudiments of learning. No log cabin had any glass windows, and if apertures were cut in the logs, it was not safe to leave them open when Indians were about.

The Americans in these early settlements in Illinois did not trespass on Indian rights, by taking their country. The Kaskaskia Indians and their allies sold this part of the Illinois country, and gave possession to the French nearly a century before the period of these depredations, and the Kickapoos, Shawanoes and other Indians, whose country was from one hundred and fifty to five hundred miles distant, committed all the murders and robberies. The Kaskaskias remained peaceable during the war, lived within the range of these settlements, in the American bottom, a few miles above the town of Kaskaskia, cultivated corn, beans, and other vegetables, and hunted in the vicinity of the white settlements.

Savage Indians have astonishing propensities for war and plunder. Before the European race came to this continent, the different nations and tribes were fighting and plundering each other, and they still keep up the practice, unless prevented by the strong arm of our national government. Nothing short of the influence of the gospel on their hearts can cure these diabolical passions.

The Indians who were hostile to the Americans did not attack the French inhabitants, for they had been accustomed to trade with them, and had been on friendly terms for half a century.

CHAPTER XI.

Religious families noticed.—Capt. Joseph Ogle.—James Lemen, Sen.—The three associates.—Upper Louisiana.—Attack on St. Louis.—The Governor a Traitor.—The assailants retire.—American immigration encouraged.—Baptists and Methodists go there.

With the religious families we have named, both Baptists and Methodists, Mr. Clark found himself at home. All were hospitable, kind and generous; no one begrudged him the comforts of life, in their frontier mode of living. As he studiously avoided making any trouble, and never appeared in the character of a preaching lounger, each family made him welcome to their homely fare. As he was more frequently the inmate of the families of Capt. Joseph Ogle, the Methodist class leader, and James Lemen, a leading Baptist in the community, it will be entertaining to our readers to have a sketch of these two pioneers.

CAPTAIN JOSEPH OGLE migrated with the Messrs. Zanes and other families, from the south branch of the Potomac to the vicinity of Wheeling in 1769, where he distinguished himself in the siege of Fort Henry, in 1777. In the summer of 1785, he moved down the Ohio river to the Illinois country, and at first settled in the American bottom, in the present county of Monroe. Being well qualified, he was chosen for a leader of the little band of pioneers, who had to defend themselves from Indian assaults. Indeed he was just such a man as the people in all exposed and frontier settlements look to as their counsellor, guide and commander. He possessed uncommon firmness and self-possession, had great energy, and yet was mild, peaceable, and kind-hearted in social intercourse; always striving for the maintenance of peace, good order and justice in the social relations. From the spring of 1784 to 1790, there was in fact no organized government in the Illinois country. Some of the forms of law were kept up, but in a truthful sense the people were "a law unto themselves," and Captain Ogle, whom every body respected, was exactly the kind of man to preserve order. Other pioneers, who had talents and influence, occupied the same position. And this too was the period of Indian alarms, and the people had to do their own fighting. What the poet says of the fictitious Rolla, applied with much pertinence to Captain Ogle—

"In war, a tiger chafed by the hunter's spear;
In peace, more gentle than the unwean'd lamb."

He was scrupulously honest, punctual and strict in the fulfillment of all his engagements, and expected from all his neighbors the same degree of honesty and punctuality. The following anecdote will furnish an illustration of his true character.

A neighbor, by the name of Sullivan, who was not quite as punctual in performing promises as he ought to have been, borrowed some house-logs of Mr. Ogle to finish his cabin, promising to cut and return as many on a certain day. Capt. Ogle had arranged to raise his own cabin the day after the logs became due, but they were not returned. He went with several men to Sullivan's cabin, told the family to remove any articles that might be in the house on the side he was about to pull down, and with handspikes proceeded with great coolness and deliberation to raise the corners and take the logs from the cabin.

The owner alarmed, came out and exclaimed, "Why, Mr. Ogle, what do you mean? Do you intend to pull down my house over my head?" "By no means, neighbor Sullivan, I am only getting out my own logs." "Now, Captain Ogle, do stop, and I will go right off to the woods and get you the logs." "Very well, Mr. Sullivan, if you will have the logs at my place to-morrow morning at sunrise, which you promised to have done to-day, I will forbear, else I shall take these logs for my cabin to-morrow." This was said with the most impassive coolness and deliberation, and Mr. Sullivan was obliged to perform a most unpleasant night's labor for slackness in his promises.

With uncommon firmness and energy, he united kindness and gentleness, and ruled the people by a happy blending of fear and love. He was always a moral man, but became a devout Christian professor from the first visit of James Smith to the time of his death, in February, 1821, at fourscore years of age. For twenty years he had resided in St. Clair county, about eight miles north of Belleville, and to this day he is spoken of by the old pioneers in the vicinity with the endearing epithet of "Grandfather Ogle." This man's house was one of the homes of Father Clark for several years.

JAMES LEMEN, Sen., who married the eldest daughter of Capt. Ogle, was another home for the pioneer preacher. There is a pleasant tradition among their descendants, relative to their earliest acquaintance. Both were young, moral persons, religiously educated, and at first sight both were impressed with the idea they were destined for each other. They were soon married, and their mutual attachment was strong, steady, and lasted through life. Not a discordant feeling, or an unpleasant word ever passed between them. His grandfather was an emigrant from the north of Ireland to Virginia, and he was born in Berkeley county in the autumn of 1760. His father belonged to the church of England (a branch of which existed in Virginia, before the revolutionary war,) but died when he was only a year old. His mother married again, and he was brought up by a strict Presbyterian. James Lemen was rigidly honest, humane, kind-hearted, and benevolent, independent in judgment, very firm and conscientious in whatever he believed to be right, and showed strong traits of decision. Though he served two years in the revolutionary army, under General Washington, he was opposed to war as an aggressive measure, never combative or cruel; yet he would fight like a hero, when impelled by a sense of duty in defending the settlement from Indian aggressions.

He followed his father-in-law to the Illinois country in the spring of 1786, by descending the Ohio river in a flat boat. The second night after he left Wheeling, the river fell while they were tied to the shore, and his boat lodged on a stump, careened and sunk, by which accident he lost all his provisions and chattels. His eldest son Robert, then a boy of three years, floated on the bed where he lay, which his father caught by the corner of the ticking, and saved his life. That boy is now a hale old man, with silvered locks, and past the age of threescore and ten, honored and beloved by all who know him.

Though left destitute of provisions and other necessaries, James Lemen was not the man to be discouraged. He had energy and perseverance, and got to the mouth of the Ohio, and from thence up the Mississippi to Kaskaskia, where he arrived on the tenth of July. His family was one of the first to form the settlement of New Design, on the old hill trace between Kaskaskia and St. Louis, and his house became the half-way stopping place for many years. No travelers were turned away.

He had been the subject of religious impressions from childhood, but was not clear in his mind to make a profession of faith in Christ, until Rev. Mr. Dodge came to the country and preached, as already stated, when he and his wife, with two other persons, were baptized.

He was generous and hospitable, and often divided his corn with the destitute. He observed the Sabbath strictly, kept good order in his family, yet was never harsh or severe with his children.

In the same settlement, and frequently for weeks in succession, at the cabin of Mr. Lemen, there was an Irish Methodist by the name of William Murray. His name indicates Scots descent, and he and Mr. Clark were quite intimate. Indeed, these three men claimed national affinity, for, as we have shown, Mr. Lemen's ancestors were from the north of Ireland, where colonies from Scotland had taken possession in the seventeenth century. There was just enough diversity in their opinions, to invite controversy, and enough Christian virtue as a controlling principle to keep them within the bounds of moderation and fraternal intercourse. They attended each others meetings, and Mr. Clark preached, and exerted an influence on the young men in the settlement that has never been lost.

We will now pass over a few months, till some time in the spring or summer of 1798, when Mr. Clark carried out his long cherished project of visiting the Spanish country west of the Mississippi river, and which made him in a peculiar sense *the pioneer preacher.*

LOUISIANA was discovered, settled, and held in possession by France until 1762, when, by a secret treaty, it was sold to Spain by that infamous king, Louis XV, and his more infamous mistress, Madame Pompadour, and his corrupt ministry. The first permanent settlement in Upper Louisiana was commenced with the founding of St. Louis as a trading post in 1764. In 1763, an enterprising trader by the name of *Pierre Ligueste Laclede*, obtained a grant from the Director General of Louisiana, with the "necessary powers to trade with the Indians of the Missouri, and those west of the Mississippi, above the Missouri river, as far north as the St. Peters," now Minnesota. A small hamlet had been previously established by a few French families, and called St. Genevieve, west of the Great River, and a few miles below the town of Kaskaskia, and some temporary stations made in the lead mine country, west of St. Genevieve.

The Spanish authority became regularly established in Upper Louisiana, in November, 1770. Piernas, the Spanish commandant, arrived in St. Louis at that date, but there is no official document or record to show that he exercised the functions of his office previous to February, 1771. Other towns or villages were settled in the vicinity from 1769, the date of St. Charles, to the period of 1780.

On the transfer of the Illinois country from France to Great Britain in 1765, many of the French inhabitants removed from that side of the river to St. Louis and St. Charles, and many more went down the river to the lower province.

After Colonel George Rogers Clark had taken possession of the Illinois country, under Virginia, in 1778, he became personally acquainted and held frequent interviews with French citizens of St. Louis, and the official authorities.

While at Cahokia, in 1779, only five miles distant, holding treaties with the Indians from confidential agents whom he sent into the Indian country northward, he learned that British agents from Canada, with a large force of northern Indians, were projecting an invasion of St. Louis. Being on terms of friendly intercourse with Governor Leyba, the Spanish commandant, he gave him intimation of these treacherous designs, as he did to several French gentlemen, and tendered his services with the forces he commanded, in case of an attack. St. Louis then was enclosed with short palisades, and gates opened in the pathways that led to the common field, and to the country without. The sequel gave proof that the governor was a traitor, purchased, doubtless, with British gold.

In the month of May, 1780, a large band of warriors from different tribes of Indians from the Upper Mississippi and the northern lakes, with a number of Canadians, amounting in all to twelve or fourteen hundred armed men, appeared in the forest east of the Mississippi, above St. Louis. The 25th of May was the festival of *Corpus Christi*, a day highly venerated by the inhabitants who were Catholics. Had the assault been made on that day it would have been fatal to the town; for after the service in the church, nearly all the inhabitants, men, women and children, flocked to the prairie to gather strawberries, which were abundant, and delicious at that season. A few Indians had crossed the river as spies, and secreted themselves in the thickets near where the people passed.

Next day the main body crossed the river, and attacked the town. A few persons who had gone to the field, were attacked from an ambuscade; some were killed; others fled to the town and gave the alarm. The soldiers under the command of the Governor, and his subalterns, either from fear or treachery, hid themselves, and the citizens alone had to defend the place. They found some government cannon, and fired grape shot as the invaders approached the gates. A few days previous the treacherous governor sold all the public ammunition to some traders, but the people supplied themselves with eight kegs of powder they found in a trader's house.

The governor kept within his house, but hearing the firing, and learning the citizens were making a manful resistance, he came out, ordered the firing to cease, and the cannon to be spiked and filled with sand by some of his minions. Fortunately the men at the lower gate did not hear the peremptory order, and continued the firing. The governor, perceiving this, ordered a cannon to be fired at them. They threw themselves on the ground, and the murderous volley of grape shot passed over their heads. This horrible procedure, with his general conduct, fixed the indelible brand of traitor on his name, and such the French citizens reported him to have been, to the immediate representative of the crown of Spain in New Orleans.

The inhabitants of St. Louis were in a critical situation. With evidence of treachery among the officers, who were Spanish; the place invaded by a force nearly double to the whole population, men, women and children; and these invaders infuriated with the spirit of war and plunder, what could they expect but a general massacre! But after killing and scalping twenty persons in the field and prairie, and meeting with such determined resistance at the gates, the Indians retired suddenly, and refused to coöperate with their Canadian allies, who kept themselves at a safe distance.

The cause of this sudden and unexpected retreat has been a mystery. The most probable solution is the tradition among the French inhabitants, that the Indians were told they were going on a war party to fight the Spaniards; but when they discovered the defenders of the town were all Frenchmen, and recognized amongst them some of their personal friends, who had lived and traded in their villages; and that they had been deceived by British agents, they withdrew in ill-humor with their employers.

Divers misstatements of this assault have been handed down by writers and oral tradition. A popular error has been propagated, that Colonel Clark was at Cahokia, (some say Kaskaskia) and suddenly appeared on the bank of the Mississippi, opposite the town with a strong force. Colonel Clark left the Illinois country with all the men whom he could persuade to re-enlist, the preceding February, went down the Mississippi, and at the date of the attack was establishing fort Jefferson, below the mouth of the Ohio. From thence he traveled on foot with a single companion through the wilderness to Harrodsburg in Kentucky.

The traditional fact of his giving information to Governor Leyba, in 1779, of the projected invasion, and the offer of aid, has caused this error. The register of the old Catholic church in St. Louis of the funeral obsequies of the persons massacred, furnishes incontestible evidence that the attack was on May 26th, 1780.

Aware that a report of his treasonable conduct had been forwarded to the Governor General at New Orleans, fearful of the consequences, and unable to sustain the scorn and indignation heaped upon him, Governor Leyba died shortly after the attack; having poisoned himself, as the creditable report was. Cartabona, his deputy, performed the functions of the office until the next year, when Don Francisco Cruzat, the predecessor of Leyba, and who had been supplanted by him in 1778, returned and assumed the command a second time.

In a few years after an important change was made in the government of Upper Louisiana, by the appointment of a commandant-general, or governor for that province, and a commandant, or lieutenant-governor for each district. The commandant-general was Don Carlos Dehault Delassus, and the lieut. governor of St. Louis district was an intelligent French gentleman of liberal principles, M. Zenon Trudeau.

We have given these facts of St. Louis history to explain why so many Americans had settled in the province before Father Clark made his first visit.

The attack on St. Louis from Canada, the detection of the meditated invasion by Colonel Clark, and the friendly intercourse between the French citizens of St. Louis and those of Illinois, induced the authorities of Louisiana to encourage the immigration of Americans from the United States to the Upper province. To this intent a movement was made by Don Guardoqui, Spanish minister to the government of the United States at Philadelphia, as early as 1787, when he proposed a plan of emigration from the western settlements to the country from Arkansas to the settlements on the Missouri.43 Instructions were given to the commandants regulating the grants of land, and the conditions of admitting this class of immigrants. Instructions were issued by Gayoso, commandant-general, the first of January, 1798, from which we give an extract.44 No settler was to be admitted in the province who was not a farmer or mechanic.

Of course practically, this included all who came. The sixth article provided for a limited degree of toleration to Protestants.

"Liberty of conscience is not to be extended beyond the first generation; the children of the emigrants must be Catholics." [This of course required their baptism in the Catholic form, but it was not enforced.] "Emigrants not agreeing to this, must not be admitted, but removed, even when they bring property with them. This is to be explained to settlers, who do not profess the Catholic religion."

We shall see in the sequel, how the liberal minded commandants interpreted this ordinance.

The seventh regulation, "Expressly recommended to the commandants to watch that *no preacher of any religion* but the Catholic, comes into the province."

After the attack on St. Louis of 1780, measures were adopted to fortify the town more effectually, and in 1794 the garrison on the hill (now Third street, or Broadway) and the Government house were completed. In 1797, apprehensions were entertained of another invasion from Canada, and four stone towers, at equal distances, in a circular direction around the town, and a wooden block-house near the lower end, were erected. But their chief dependence for protection was the American emigrants who had been invited into the province by the liberal policy of grants of land, and the indulgence shown by the commandants. They were permitted to locate themselves in the country, and make farms, whereas the French families were required to live in villages, and cultivate their farms near by under an enclosure in common. At the transfer of the country in 1804, more than three-fifths of the inhabitants of Upper Louisiana were English Americans from the United States.45

The Roman Catholic faith was the established religion of the province. American immigrants were examined by the commandants as to their faith, but by the use of a pious fiction on the part of the examiners, and the provision in the ordinances already quoted, large toleration actually existed.

The mode of examination gave great latitude for Protestants to come in. A few general and rather equivocal questions were asked, which persons of almost any Christian sect could consistently answer; such as, "Do you believe in Almighty God?—In the Holy Trinity?—In the true, apostolical church?—In Jesus Christ our Saviour?—In the holy evangelists? etc. An affirmative answer being given to these and other questions of a general character, "*Un bon Catholique*," (a good Catholic) closed the ceremony.

Many Baptists, Methodists, and other Protestant families, settled in the province, and remained undisturbed in their religious principles. Much the largest proportion of American Protestants came into the country after 1794. They held no religious meetings publicly, and had no minister of the gospel among them. There were about fifty persons who had been members of Protestant churches in the United States, in the districts of St. Louis and St. Charles, at the period of Mr. Clark's first visit, besides as many more in the districts of St. Genevieve, and Cape Girardeau.

The Catholic priests of Upper Louisiana received from the Spanish treasury a stipend rating from $350 to $400 a year, besides the perquisites for mass, confessions, marriages, and funerals. No tithes were levied in Louisiana, and hence Protestants and free-thinkers felt no burdens in pecuniary demands from the priesthood. There were three curates, one vicar, and a few missionary priests who resided in the upper province. The rite of marriage must be performed by a Catholic priest; and it is probable the administration of baptism, or the Lord's supper, by a Protestant, would have sent him to prison, but no minister made the attempt.

The American settlers in general were peaceable, industrious, moral and well disposed persons, who, from various motives, had crossed the "Great River;" some from love of adventure—some from that spirit of restlessness that animates a numerous class of Americans—but a larger number went with the expectation of obtaining grants of land, for the trifling expense of surveying and recording the plat. We have been personally acquainted with many of these emigrants, conversed with them freely, knew their character well, and have heard so many of them declare their expectation that in due time the country would be annexed to the United States, that we have no doubt such an impression did exist largely. Yet they projected no *filibustering* enterprise; no schemes of a revolution; nor were there amongst them any sanguine spirits at work to excite such feelings.

From the time of the definitive treaty of 1783, the government of the United States had been negociating with Spain for the free navigation of the Mississippi river to the ocean, secured, as was understood, by that treaty. The inhabitants west of the Alleghany mountains were deeply interested in such a measure. It was a topic of conversation in all circles, and discussed freely in the newspapers. It is not strange that the public mind in this valley should entertain the conviction that by some form of negociation the country would be annexed to the American Union. They did not realize that a removal to the west of the great river would expatriate them and their posterity, nor did they lose their attachment to the Republic by a residence in the dominions of the crown of Spain.

Such was the character, and such were the circumstances of the people to whom Mr. Clark was the *pioneer preacher*. Certainly, no minister of the gospel, in the scriptural sense of that term, ever passed the boundary before him. He visited the American families from house to house, in a quiet and peaceable manner, conversed and prayed with them, and was received with great cordiality. There were men and women, disciples of Christ, who had not heard the precious gospel for a long period. A few gathered, on the Sabbath, in some log cabin, with fearful forebodings. They might be arrested, and, with the preacher, sent to the *calabozo*,46 or to the Mexican mines for their heretical practices. A larger number came out stealthily by night. Mr. Clark found the American families dispersed over the country, for some miles distant, and living in log cabins of the most primitive sort. Of the Baptists who were pioneers to this country before Mr. Clark, we can call to recollection the names of Abraham and Sarah Musick; Abraham Musick, Jun., as he was called, to distinguish him from his uncle, and Terrell, his wife; Adam and Lewis Martin, who were brothers, and their wives; Mr. Richardson and wife; Mrs. Jane Sullens; Sarah Williams, (who lived to see her son and four grandsons ministers of the Gospel); Mrs. Whitley, all in St. Louis district; and David Darst and wife, William Hancock and wife, Mr. Brown and family, and several others, who settled in the district of St. Charles, north of the Missouri river. There were three settlements in the district (now county) of St. Louis, where, after two or three casual visits, Mr. Clark made regular appointments, and crossed the river monthly. These were the settlement near the Spanish pond, north of St. Louis; the settlement between Owen's station (now Bridgton) and Florrissant; and the settlement called Feefe's creek.47 He was threatened repeatedly with the *calabozo*, for violating the laws of the country. M. Trudeau, the lieutenant-governor of St. Louis district, was a liberalist in principle, who, with his parents, had been driven out of France by the storm of the revolution, and their estate confiscated. He obtained the appointment of deputy commandant, through the influence of the principal French citizens, as the means of sustaining his aged parents, who had suffered for their loyalty. He abhorred all kinds of persecution, but, in his official station, in accordance with the ordinances, he was compelled "to watch that no preacher of any religion but the Catholic came into the province."

Abraham Musick, Jun., who had formed a friendly acquaintance with the lieut. governor, and, in their social interviews, had given him information of the distinctive principles of the Baptists, as contradistinguished from the Catholic and Protestant Pædo-Baptists, made application to M. Trudeau for liberty to hold meetings in his house. We give the colloquy in substance as we received it from the pious and intelligent widow of Mr. M——, twenty-five years after the interview.

M. "My friend, John Clark, is in the country, on a visit to his friends. He is a good man, peaceably disposed, and will behave as a good citizen should. The American people desire to hear him preach at my house occasionally. Will the commandant please give permission, that we may not be molested? We will hold our meetings quietly, make no disturbance, and say nothing against the king of Spain, nor the Catholic religion."

The commandant was inclined to favor the American settlers, but he was obliged to reject all such petitions officially, and replied, with seeming determination:

C. "No, Monsieur Musick. I can not permit no such ting; 'tis against de law; you must all be *bon Catholique* in dis contree. Very sorry, Mons. Musick, I cannot oblige you, but I must follow de 'Regulacion.'"

Discouraged at this decision, in a tone so magisterial, Mr. M. regarded any farther effort hopeless, and arose to depart from the office, when, with a gracious countenance, the commandant said:

"Sit down, Mons. Musick; please sit down; I soon get dis paper fix for dese gentlehomme who wait; and den we talk. You must eat my dinner, and drink a glass of my *bon vin*. You and I are good friend, though I cannot let you make a church house."

After dispatching the business on hand, M. Trudeau insisted on the company of Mr. Musick to dinner. While discoursing with volubility in his imperfect English, the wily commandant adverted to the petition, so unceremoniously rejected in the office.

C. "You understand me, Monsieur Musick, I presume. You must not put—what do you call him—*un colcher*,48 on your house and call it a *church*;—dat is all wrong,—you must make no bell ring. And now hear me, Mons. Musick, you must let no man baptize your *enfant* but de parish priest. But if your friend come to see you—your neighbor come there,—you *conversez*;—you say prayer;—you read Bible—you sing song—dat is all right—you all *bon Catholique*."

Mr. Clark from the time he left Georgia had been reading the Scriptures, to find out the character of a church, such as those congregations named in Jerusalem, Antioch, Ephesus, Corinth, etc. He was then a Baptist so far as infant baptism was concerned, and he doubted much whether any uninspired human authority could change the form approved by Christ, without destroying the institution. And the majority of the people, being Baptists, had no use for the parish priest for that ceremony. The interdiction of spire and bell was no inconvenience in their simple form of worship. Unlike the Catholic, their religion had no connection with bell-ringing.

While this disposition of a perplexing question to the commandant accommodated the American settlers, it gave no legal countenance to the visits of a preacher from another nation, and a different religion,—but the people came out to the meetings with less fear of the prison. Mr. Clark continued his visits nearly every month, which did not escape the notice of the commandant. He soon learned the period of his visits, and some two or three days before his return to Illinois, he never failed to send a threatening message into the country that, "If Mons. Clark did not leave the Spanish country in three days, he would be put in the *calabozo*." So regularly came this message that it became a standing jest with his friends to enquire, "Well, brother Clark, when do you go to the *calabozo*?" "In three days," would be the reply, which all understood to mean crossing the river to the Illinois side.

In the autumn of 1801, Rev. Thomas R. Musick, a relative of the Musick families, came to the province on a visit. His residence then was in the Green river district in Kentucky, and he had been in a revival of religion for several months, and about one hundred converts had been baptized. His brother was the one who petitioned the commandant for privilege to hold meetings, and his uncle was one of the residents in the Spanish country. Coming from the midst of an extensive and powerful revival of religion, he was in the spirit of preaching, and cared little for the Spanish calabozo. He visited every family, in which professors of religion were to be found, in the districts of St. Louis and St. Charles, and during three weeks' sojourn, preached fifteen times to congregations assembled in log cabins and in the woods, on short notice to hear him. He was threatened with the calabozo repeatedly. In a frontier settlement above St. Charles, he preached the funeral sermon of a Baptist by name of Brown, from Kentucky, who had died there that season.

Mr. Musick left the province with the determination to return with his family and settle there, soon as he could be permitted to remain and preach the gospel; and with this end in view, he removed to the settlement of New Design in Illinois.

Soon as the news of the cession of the country to the United States reached his ears, without waiting for its confirmation by the government, and the actual transfer, he went across the great river in the autumn of 1803, and made that country his home. Mr. Musick was the first preacher of the gospel who, with his family, settled in the country, became one of the constituents of Fefee's Creek, and was its pastor for more than thirty years.

CHAPTER XII.

Forms a Methodist Class in Illinois.—Gradual change of Views.—Mode of Inquiry.—Circumstances of his Baptism.—Practical progress in Baptist Principles.—Zeal and influence in promoting education.—Early Schools in the Illinois country.—A formidable obstruction to a pupil.—Three fellows in the way.—Want of books.—A whiskey-loving teacher rightly served.—Effects of Father Clark's teaching.—Visits Kentucky again.—Visits to West Florida.—Interview with a Sick man.—Efficacy of Prayer.—A Revolution.

We shall now confine our attention entirely to Father Clark. Soon after he began his regular visits to the Spanish country, he gathered into a society a small class of disciples, and held regular meetings with them near Bellefontaine, some three or four miles north of New Design. He still regarded himself a Methodist, though independent of that ecclesiastical connection. He was scarcely conscious at that period, that he was gradually diverging from the peculiarities of Wesleyism and approaching the fundamental principles of Baptist faith and practice. He had held his intellect and conscience open to conviction from the time he left the conference in Georgia, by the prayerful resolve to follow the Scriptures, and bring all his religious practice into strict conformity to that divine rule. His habit of praying in every perplexity, until his mind became satisfied that he was in the pathway of duty, continued and increased with advancing years. At the same time, as ever after, he was liberal to all other Christians, and made no efforts to proselyte them to his own peculiar views. He explained the Scriptures, and urged on all whom he addressed in public, or conversed with in private, the duty of studying the Word of God, and following wherever it led. Christ was ever held up as sole law-giver in Zion. For several years the conviction had increased that he was unbaptized, and that by this ordinance more than any other, the disciples of Christ made a profession of faith in him. He had become convinced that the ceremony performed in unconscious infancy, by virtue of some mystical covenant relationship of his parents, and by the pastor of the church where he was born, was to him no part of Christian obedience.

In the little society he had gathered was a good man by the name of Talbot, who had been a local Methodist preacher. Mr. Clark and this man became quite intimate. Both had about the same views of Christian ordinances and a gospel church state. Mr. Talbot regarded himself unbaptized, and repeatedly requested baptism from the hands of his brother. We have repeatedly shown that Father Clark was subject to very serious impressions of mind concerning his duty, made it a subject of fervent prayer, and was conscientious not to resist the impressions he felt in answer to prayer. His judgment had become clear on the scriptural form of baptism, but who should baptize him was with him a momentous question. After another season of private prayer, the conviction was felt that he must baptize Talbot, and Talbot administer the same ordinance to him. And so it happened. A meeting was appointed at Fountain Creek, a small stream that still meanders among the hills in Monroe county, where a large congregation, compared to the present population of the country, came out. After preaching, and a relation of their religious experience, views of the kingdom and ordinances of Jesus Christ, they both went down into the water, and Mr. Talbot baptized Father Clark, and Clark baptized Talbot, and then baptized several other persons.

If a regular and uninterrupted succession of baptisms from the days of the apostles is indispensable to qualify the administrator, and give validity to the ordinance, then there was certainly a broken link in the chain here, as there was in that of Roger Williams and Deacon Holliman. He who thinks he is in possession of such an unbroken chain is bound to show every link. Assertions and imaginings are not historical proofs.

At the next regular meeting, a month later, Mr. Clark again baptized two or three others of his society, one of whom, a venerable and pious member of the Methodist society, yet lives within the vicinity of the writer. Both Mr. Clark and Mr. Talbot, were regular administrators of religious ordinances according to Pædobaptist usage, for they had been duly authorized by the Methodist Episcopal church, had left that connection in an orderly mode, and still sustained the ministerial office. It was ten or twelve years after this before he became regularly connected with the Baptist denomination.

Amongst his other services that implanted him in the confidence and affections of the people, was his ability, zeal and influence in the cause of education. In this department of labor, as in his gospel ministrations, he engaged from no personal or pecuniary motives. His services were offered to all who would come under his tuition and behave properly. For his board and clothing, he relied on the liberality of his patrons. He was in fact *the pioneer teacher* in this country, for all before him were unfit for that business.

In the French villages, common school education was neglected. Some of the priests and elderly females taught the children the elements of their religion, and to read their native language, but a large proportion of that class of people grew up to manhood with little knowledge of science and literature, and less learning.

The first school ever taught among the American settlers in the Illinois country, was by Solomon Seely, in 1783. Francis Clark, an intemperate man, came next, and had a small school in Moore's settlement near Bellefontaine, in 1785. He did quite as much harm as good. Next after him for two or three years was an insignificant Irishman by name of Halfpenny. He possessed very little learning and less skill in teaching. School books were scarce and more difficult of attainment than in Kentucky. Each pupil carried such a book from which to say his lessons, as could be found in his father's log cabin. One little fellow, whose memory was not in the best order and his perceptive faculties slow of development, had the Bible for his book for "easy readings." Master Halfpenny had no more schoolmaster sense than to give out his lessons from the book of Daniel, and third chapter. Partly by spelling out the words, and partly by the aid of a school-fellow, he had made tolerable progress in pronouncing the "hard words" and proper names through eleven verses. In the twelfth verse he met the formidable obstruction of the three Hebrew names, Shadrach, Meshach, and Abednego, which he could not surmount. The master was petulant, surly, and uttered a series of strange sounds, in jabbering Irish, which the poor afflicted pupil could neither understand nor imitate. He did his very best to pronounce these names in the way the master ordered, and was dismissed with the formidable threat of a striped jacket the next day if he forgot them. Next day came, and the little fellow was in his seat, toiling at his lesson, for he really tried to learn. His turn came to "say his lesson," and he stood beside the master in a tremor that shook his little frame and the perspiration streaming down his cheeks. His lesson commenced with the thirteenth verse. Nebuchadnezzar was one of those long words that had gone round the school on divers occasions, and little Tommy, as he was familiarly called in the family circle, had mastered that before the stupid master had put him into the book of Daniel. He read two lines distinctly with a tremulous voice, for the threat of a striped jacket had not escaped his memory, when he stopped suddenly. "Th'read on," sounded in his ears like the crack of the hazle;—"why don't ye th'read on, ye spalpeen," came again with the expectation of the whip. The trembling pupil, unable to recollect or repeat any thing, burst into tears and sobs, and made an effort to explain his inability—"Why here are these three fellows again, and I don't know them." Master Halfpenny for once was disarmed. There was so much simplicity and honest effort in the boy that the master made a kind effort to relieve his pupil. "Why, boy, cannot ye mind th'em? They ar' *Mister Shaderack, Mes-hack, and Abed-ye-go.* Now ye mought go on with y'r lesson; and don't ye miss 'em agin."

Spelling, reading, writing and the mere elements of simple arithmetic were all that these and many others pretended to teach. The difficulties encountered in obtaining a small amount of education by children in Illinois, from the earliest American settlements to the close of the last century were greater, and books more difficult to be procured than when Mr. Clark taught in Kentucky. The price of a single copy of "Dilworth's New Guide to the English Tongue," as the title page read, was one dollar. And none but old copies of the coarsest paper, the refuse of old stores and printing offices, sold at auction, were brought to this remote frontier. No classes were organized, nor could there be any uniformity of books. The masters ruled, not with "a rod of iron," but a wand of hickory, four feet long. The teachers were turned out at Christmas, when the king of misrule took the chair, and lawlessness prevailed. Not only were the scenes enacted, we described in chapter ninth, in Kentucky, but even more lamentable and ludicrous ones.

A few years later, one of the whiskey-loving sons of Erin attempted to teach in a settlement known to the writer, who received the tale from one of the employers. Our informant, who loved his dram, despised all meanness and selfishness, and he regarded a man who would "suck a jug" in secret, as about the meanest of the race. Hence he "abominated" the schoolmaster, and gloried in the tricks some of the youngsters played him. The master was observed by the shrewd young men under his charge, to retire from the cabin to a thicket during the hours for lessons, and in proportion to these occasions of retirement, his eyes grew dull, his tongue wagged heavily, and his natural jabbering as an Irish pedagogue, became more unintelligible.

A search warrant in a verbal form was issued and served on the thicket by two smart young men; the whiskey bottle was found, and in quite a private way received a full allowance of tartar-emetic, and then carefully deposited in its accustomed hiding place. Next day the master was seized suddenly with an alarming illness. It would have been called cholera, but that disease was unknown on these frontiers at that period. But, as our informant expressed it, "he was orfully skeered, and glad enough to have us let him off from his article."

Mr. Clark taught the youngsters about Bellefountaine, New Design, and the "Bottom," at various intervals for eight or ten years. Though other teachers met with the customary Christmas frolic, and were dethroned, Mr. Clark was an exception. Not one of the roguish young men in the settlements would offer him such an insult. Those pupils who were kept under proper government at home, made no trouble in the school. But there were wild and rude young lads, who were devoid of self-respect, and required the application of the hazel and hickory. One of our old friends, now past the age of threescore and ten, was a student of Mr. Clark, at times, for several years, and received ample qualifications under his tuition for the official duties of marshall under the territorial government, and who also has been a useful teacher. Of him we have made special inquiry how he managed these insubordinate youngsters, and how their rebellious habits affected his temper and patience. His response is, that on some occasions he thought him to be slightly irritated, that occasionally he had to use the rod, that he would have order in his school, and that he always discriminated between criminality and dullness.49 The modern contrivances for teaching arithmetic and the elements of mathematics were then unknown. The rules were written out by the teacher, and the sums when worked right were all copied in a book. Not long since we looked over a book preserved by another student, with the date of 1806, then twenty-one, now verging to seventy years of age.50 A third, and one who for almost half a century, has been esteemed as one of our ablest and most successful ministers, (as has also his brother just named,) acknowledges himself as having received special aid from this pioneer preacher in preparing him for the ministry. This person in earlier life performed a prominent part in the public affairs of the territorial and state governments. In addition to minor branches, he studied mathematics, logic, rhetoric, history and philosophy. This minister, as several others have done, acknowledges his indebtedness to Father Clark for his valuable aid in those branches specially relating to the profession of the ministry.51 Many others who shared the benefits of his instruction have long since followed their beloved teacher to "that bourne from whence no traveler returns."

Mr. Clark made a visit to Kentucky before the period of his baptism, but what year we find no one who can recollect. It was probably about 1800, or 1801, during the period of the great revivals there, for he had large congregations wherever he preached, and unusual success followed. He was absent several months, and his friends in Illinois were anxious for his return, and sent William Murray as a messenger through the wilderness to recall him. Mr. Murray came into a crowded congregation, soon after Mr. Clark had commenced his sermon. While his quick eyes were glancing over the deeply affected congregation, they lit on the well known form and features of the messenger, and a suspicion of his errand flashed on his mind.

"There's brother Murray, from the Illinois country, and no doubt the Lord has sent him for me to return there. I had an impression this morning in prayer that I must go back to that destitute field. Try to get a seat, brother Murray, and wait patiently, for I must finish my sermon. It is probably the last time I shall ever preach in Kentucky, and I can't leave without warning poor sinners once more to flee to the Saviour."

There was nothing extravagant in this style of address. In that congregation, it would have turned no one's thoughts from the subject. It is no unusual thing for ministers, while preaching, to throw out a parenthetical sentence to individuals present, and receive responses. It causes no interruption to persons who are not tied up by forms, and restrained by conventionalities, as in older communities.

The meeting continued till a late hour that day. Anxious persons desired instruction, and Father Clark was called on repeatedly to offer prayers for sinners in distress. Then the congregation must sing some familiar songs, give him the hand of fellowship, and beg him to remember them in his prayers when far away. Next morning Mr. Clark and his friend were on the trail for the Illinois country.

It was about the year 1807 or '08, that Mr. Clark, after a long season of prayer and impressions, went down the Mississippi river on a mission to West Florida.52 The tract of country, exclusive of the Island of Orleans, now belonging to the State of Louisiana, and called West Florida, was retained by the Spanish government, after the cession of Louisiana, though understood by both the French and American governments to be included in that cession. The laws of Spain and the Catholic religion existed in that district. Baton Rouge was the site of a Spanish fort, in which a small garrison was stationed. A large part of the population were emigrants from the south-western States, and claimed the right of transfer with the people of Louisiana. They made an unsuccessful effort to throw off the Spanish yoke in 1805. In this district, and amongst these Americans, Mr. Clark spent several months, preaching and teaching. The towns of Baton Rouge53 and Bayon Sara were on the river, and the settlements in the country extended over the district of East Feliciana. Mr. Clark made a second visit to this country about 1810, or '11, and we can give several incidents that occurred, but cannot distinguish on which tour. On his first voyage he started in a small canoe from the Merimac river in St. Louis county, and Mr. Boly, one of his friends, aided in fitting him out. To balance the frail craft in which he embarked, poles of light papaw wood were lashed across the canoe. In this light vessel thus trimmed he floated with the current, and steered with a single paddle by day, and encamped in the dense forest that lined the shore at night. The voyage of more than one thousand miles, down this turbid, foaming river, was made in safety. He was alone, and yet not alone, for a deep conviction of the all-seeing and everywhere-present God rested on his mind wherever he traveled, by night and by day. Through the Mediator and mercy seat he held communion, habitually, with the Father of spirits, and felt the most childlike confidence in his gracious arm for protection.

It was while on one of his excursions to Florida, that he heard of the illness of a Mr. Todd, with whom he had some acquaintance in the Illinois country. Mr. Todd had gone down the river on a flat-boat with a load of produce, which he had sold out, and with one of his companions, was making the long and perilous journey on foot to the upper country. This was the common mode of transportation *down* the great rivers of this valley to market before the period of steam navigation. Flat-boats never return up the strong current, but are sold and broken up for old lumber, and the men return through the Indian country and intervening forest on foot. This was a perilous business, and caused great destruction of human life. Many perished of whom their friends never learned the particulars. Bands of robbers roamed through this wilderness, and doubtless many a farmer from Tennessee, Kentucky, and the country along the Ohio and Wabash rivers, who never returned, was murdered for the money he attempted to transport.

Mr. Todd belonged to a family in Illinois who were infidels of the Paine creed. That is, they believed in Almighty God, as the creator and governor of the world, but disbelieved the supernatural birth, divine nature and office-work of Jesus Christ as a mediator, and the divine authority of the Scriptures. Mr. Clark found Mr. Todd very sick with the bilious fever, nursed him, and continued with him until he thought himself able to travel. While at the worst stage of the disease, the sick man was given over, and thought himself he must die in that dreary wilderness, and desired Mr. Clark to pray for him. This was done repeatedly in his presence, and the preacher became unusually exercised, and spent some time in secret prayer for him, that God would spare his life, and enable him to reach his friends in the Illinois country. As Mr. Todd was about to depart on foot, with his traveling companion, for a long journey through the wilderness and Indian country, under great despondency, and with faint hopes of reaching the end of his journey, Father Clark again prayed with him, gave him encouragement, and assured him that the GOOD ONE, as he denominated our Heavenly Father, would not leave him to perish in the wilderness. He felt assured of a gracious answer to his prayers on his behalf, and that he would reach his friends, though a thousand miles lay between them.

It was a terrible affair for a sick man to travel through the swamps, cane-brakes and pine forests, and cross the rivers and creeks that lay in the route. On several occasions the sick man, in despair of reaching the end of his journey, lay down to die, when the recollection of the prayers of Father Clark, and the assurance he gave of seeing home, inspired him with new vigor, and urged him onward. He reached his brother's house in the American bottom, under the firm conviction that his life had been spared, and preternatural strength given him in answer to the prayers of that good man.

This man's constitution was broken down. He lingered along in a feeble condition, and in a year or two died of a pulmonary disease. While on his death-bed at his brother's house, (who, though he possessed some fine traits of character, remained a hardened infidel,) he sent for a minister of the gospel to visit and pray with him.54 He had previously told his friends how he had experienced the efficacy of the prayers of Mr. Clark, and he again repeated the story to his visitor, and stated with great frankness that he had serious doubts of the Bible being a revelation from God, but he had no doubt that God did hear and answer the prayers of good men.

The visiting minister, as was his habit in all such instances, conferred with the infidel brother in whose house he was, and with whom he had been personally acquainted for many years. "Mr. Todd, your brother appears to be failing. He has not long to live with us. I know your principles, that you do not believe in the Scriptures as a revelation from God, nor in Jesus Christ as a Saviour. This is your house, and I desire to do nothing that appears obtrusive. If I pray with your brother as he requests, I must pray in the name of Jesus Christ. This may be offensive to you." Mr. Todd replied, "Mr. L., my brother wishes you to pray for him. I desire you to exercise your own privilege in my house as freely as if it were your own. In every thing I desire my brother to be gratified while he lives, and I think with him that the prayers of good men are heard. I know he cannot live long."

A portion of Scripture was read, a hymn sung, and all the household kneeled around the bed, and behaved with decorum, while the minister made his petition to the throne of grace for the dying sinner.

No good, but much injury has resulted from the assumption of ministerial dignity and authority, with such people as the Todd family. Nothing is lost but much gained by courtesy and condescension. Such were the lessons taught and the example set by the successful pioneer whose life we are tracing.

In one instance, if not in both, Mr. Clark returned on foot from West Florida to the Illinois country through the intervening wilderness. His second tour was made by land, and on foot, and he preached wherever settlements existed, and left a series of appointments, which he filled on his return. In the Arkansas country he attempted to reach a settlement, but got lost in the woods and cane-brakes, and wandered for some hours without finding the signs of a human habitation. He was a thorough woodsman, but he despaired of finding the way out by his own skill. Believing in the constant protection of Divine providence, which he could obtain by prayer, he knelt down by a large tree, and continued to pray until his mind became calm, and he felt relieved of all perturbation and anxiety. Pursuing the direction to which he was led by the impressions of mind he received, he soon came to a path that led him to a house on the border of the settlement he was trying to find.

West Florida became revolutionized in 1810, and if we rightly conjecture, at the time or just before the second visit of Father Clark. That portion of Florida that lay west of the Perdido river, was originally a part of Louisiana, but the Spanish government held possession, and the government of the United States, desirous of avoiding collision with Spain, did not take forcible possession of this district. In the summer of 1810, the people of the territory, aided by their friends from Mississippi, effected a successful revolution, with very little bloodshed. A party of French, headed by Captain George Depassau, and a party of Americans, commanded by Captain H. Thomas, made a bold and successful attack on the fort at Baton Rouge, which surrendered at discretion, and the civil and military authorities of Spain were permitted to retire to Pensacola. In October the district was annexed to the United States, by the proclamation of the President, announcing that William C. C. Clairborne, governor of the territory of Orleans, was empowered to take possession of West Florida, in the name of the United States, as a portion of the territory under his jurisdiction.

While on a visit to this district in 1842, we found persons who had heard Father Clark preach, and remembered him as a pioneer school teacher.

On his return from his second tour, he was taken sick, and continued in a feeble condition for some time. His friends in St. Louis county hearing of his situation, went after him, and there being no carriage roads, they hauled him on a sled, dragged by a single horse, through the wilderness to the settlements near St. Louis.

CHAPTER XIII.

Baptists, "Friends to Humanity."—Their Anti-slavery position.—Mr. Clark joins them.—Manner of his reception.—His Views of African Slavery.—Views of African Colonization.—Made Life-member of a Colonization Society.—Circulars on Slavery.—Personal behavior.—Conversational Gifts.—Writes Family Records.

A class of Baptists had commenced organizing churches, first in Illinois and then in Missouri, denominated, as a kind of distinction from other Baptists, as "Friends to Humanity." They were frequently called emancipators by others. They were opposed to slavery, and being desirous of operating in a quiet and peaceful manner against the commerce in human beings, this class adopted rules by which they were to be governed in the admission of slave-holders into the churches. The organization originated in Kentucky, in 1807, and made a division in a small association in Illinois in 1809. They would not receive persons to membership "whose practice appeared friendly to perpetual slavery;" that is, those who justified the holding of human beings as property, on the same grounds of right as they claimed their horses or other kinds of property. They did admit to membership in the churches of Christ slave-holders under the following exceptions.

1. Persons holding young slaves, and recording a deed of emancipation at such an age as the church should agree to.

2. Persons who had purchased slaves in their ignorance, and who are willing the church should decide when they shall be free.

3. Women who have no legal power to liberate slaves.

4. Those that held slaves who from age, debility, insanity, or idiotcy were unfit for emancipation. And they add, "some other cases which we would wish the churches to judge of, agreeable to the principles of humanity."

These Baptists differed widely from modern abolitionists of the Northern States and England, at least in the following particulars.

1. They never adopted the dogma that slave-holding is a "sin *per se*,"—a sin in itself, irrespective of all the circumstances in which the parties might be providentially placed. Hence they could consistently buy slaves and prepare them for freedom; or contribute funds to enable slaves to purchase themselves, with a clear conscience.

2. They never aided fugitive slaves to escape from their masters, or secreted them, in violation of the constitution and laws of the land.

3. They never interfered in any objectionable way, with the legal and political rights of slave-holders. They preached the gospel in an acceptable and successful manner among slave-holders.

4. They aimed to do good both to master and servant, in a quiet, lawful and peaceable mode.

5. They endeavored to consult the true interests of all parties concerned.

6. They ever upheld the constitution and laws of the country in a peaceful way. Some of this class were chosen to official stations in both the territory and state of Illinois, and took the oath to support the constitution and laws of the United States without quibbling and evasion.

Their general faith and practice corresponded with the principles of Baptists in general Union.

Mr. Clark had gradually become a Baptist in all respects. For eight or ten years after he had been baptized in the manner already described, he remained in an independent position. With the exception of his visits to the lower country, the larger portion of his time he spent on the western side of the Mississippi, with occasional visits to his Illinois friends. The members that remained of the society he organized near Bellefontaine in Illinois, had attached themselves to other churches,—some to the Baptists, and others to the Methodist Episcopal church. Those about the Spanish pond and Coldwater settlements in St. Louis county gradually became Baptists, and regarded him as their pastor and spiritual guide. For some years he watched the course of his old friends, the Lemens' and others of that class. He felt deeply interested in their anti-slavery position. Their quiet, unobtrusive method of managing the perplexing question of slavery corresponded with his own views and experience. The father, his old friend and associate, had become an ordained minister, and two of his sons, who had studied under Mr. Clark, were now heads of families, and joint pastors of Cantine, (now Bethel) church, and, with their compeers in the ministry, were performing much itinerant service in the destitute settlements. Benjamin, the eldest son of Captain Joseph Ogle, was an ordained minister in this connection of Baptists. Father Clark and these brethren had always enjoyed fraternal intercourse, though no formal church connection had been formed. His manners were so inoffensive, his labors in the ministry were so disinterested and unremitting, his views were so scriptural, and his daily conduct so fully exemplified a life of faith on the Son of God, that no one thought of calling in question his regular standing in the ministry. He might have lived and died without reproach, and enjoyed the confidence of all good men in the same isolated position he had occupied from 1796. But his sound judgment guided him, and the impressions received in prayer prompted him to unite with others in a formal association. He was fearful he might set an example for erratic preachers to follow.

This class of Baptists held an annual meeting within the bounds of their churches on each returning autumn, though they had not assumed the form of a regular association. Such a meeting Mr. Clark attended, with some of the brethren from Coldwater, and proposed union and coöperation. Not from any necessity of knowing more of his character, but as a precedent for subsequent cases he was examined on his Christian experience, views of doctrine, and practice. The result being highly satisfactory, he was received by the hand of fellowship being given by all the brethren present, while an appropriate hymn was sung.

His views on African slavery gradually acquired firmness and consistency. We have traced his convictions on this subject to his exquisite sense of human rights, his innate principles of natural liberty, his sympathies with afflicted and oppressed humanity, his own deprivation of liberty by the British press-gang, and his imprisonment for nineteen months by the Spaniards in Havana. In a personal acquaintance of fifteen years, and the examination of various fugitive papers, we find no confusion of thought, and no lack of just conceptions of the subject. His intercourse with slave-holders was ever courteous and kind. He never obtruded his opinions where no good impressions could be made, nor in any way disguised his sentiments before any person. His frankness and candor were so well known, that all classes had entire confidence in his motives and mode of treating this subject.

When the subject of the colonization of free colored persons in Africa was brought to his mind by the formation of the American Colonization Society, he hailed it as an omen of good. He understood the strong objections to the emancipation of slaves remaining amongst us. He understood well the prejudices against the peculiarities of the African race, as one of the barriers to amalgamation with white people, and amidst the gloom that surrounded the hopeless bondage of that race, he saw one luminous spot in the moral hemisphere. The star of hope appeared to him to arise in Africa. The finger of providence pointed in that direction, and he abounded in faith and prayer for success in the enterprise. He was not so visionary as to imagine there would be no defects in its management, or no drawbacks in the colonization movement. He well understood it was an object not to be accomplished in one generation, and that its influence upon emancipation must be gradual and indirect. He desired to have an influence produced in the minds of slave-holders towards the moral and religious interests of the slaves.

So long known and so well understood were his anti-slavery principles, and his interest in the colonization scheme as the means of removing one of the most formidable obstructions to emancipation, that the ladies of Lofton's prairie, then in Greene, (now Jersey) county, Illinois, one of his monthly preaching stations, paid him the compliment of making him a life member of the county auxiliary society.[55]

Mr. Clark wrote several circulars for the annual association of Baptists, to which he belonged, on the subject of Slavery, which were published in their minutes. They were dictated by a courteous and christian-like spirit, plain, pointed, impressive and efficacious.

After he joined the Baptists, his labors were the same as before, except in a wider range of traveling, and more extended christian intercourse. No time was wasted in idleness or frivolous pursuits. Always cheerful, always the same devout, praying man. There were two or three families in Missouri, as Upper Louisiana was called from the period of the organization of the territory in 1812, where he made his *home*. All his earthly wants were cheerfully provided for by his friends. Certain mothers in Israel vied with each other in providing his annual supply of clothing; the domestic manufacture of their own wheels and looms. The cloth was the same as was then worn by the farmers of the country, but was kept by the wearer in a neat and tidy manner. He did not live to enter on the era of this frontier, when dress, equipages, furniture, and houses, as in the old states, were used for the special benefit of other people's eyes. Nor at that period would rank, or social position be detected by the dress a man or woman wore.

Mr. Clark was noted for refinement and simplicity. His personal appearance and dress were noticed for neatness. His habits, of which he scarcely appeared conscious, were those of the gentleman. Though he used tobacco, he never acquired the filthy practice, still very common in this country by rude and ill-mannered young men, of spitting about the fire place, stove, and furniture. If he had occasion to discharge the saliva, he invariably stepped to the door, though it might have been in a log cabin. He used the bath frequently by resorting to some retired spot in the creek or river. For many years, and until the close of life, he bathed his feet in cold water at all seasons of the year. We have known him walk a quarter of a mile, in extreme cold weather in the winter, to a spring or creek that he might lave his feet and wade in the cold water. Long practice made this habit a luxury.[56]

In all his personal intercourse, and manner of address, one could perceive not only good breeding, but a nice sense of propriety. His visits in families were no less effective in moral cultivation, than his public preaching, though that was impressive and interesting, and the instruction given highly scriptural and evangelical. He possessed a gift not very common, and probably little cultivated by ministers, in introducing the subject of personal religion, in a pleasant, conversational way.

A stranger, on witnessing his mode, would have seen nothing ministerial, dignified, or professional. There was no change in the tones of his voice, and effort made to introduce a subject not relished by the party. There was no affectation of concern for others, no cant, nothing in style or mode that differed from his conversation on ordinary topics. Young persons, unused to be addressed on such a subject, soon found themselves in the presence of a familiar friend. No man could make a more touching appeal to the mother of a young family, and while he awakened her maternal feelings to the moral and eternal welfare of her offspring, he scarcely failed impressing on her own conscience concern for her personal salvation.

It was a pleasure to him, and a gratification to the families he visited, to write out the family record in his peculiarly neat and correct chirography, in the household Bible. And when a new Bible was purchased, its possessors waited many weeks, and even months, until FATHER CLARK, as every one familiarly called him, visited them and made the record. These Bibles are preserved to this day, and may be found among the descendants of the pioneer families, dispersed as they are over a wide extent of territory. The first immigrants to Iowa, and several families who went to Oregon, carried these copies as choice memorials of a much venerated man.

For the last fifteen years of his life there was so much uniformity in his labors, that were we to follow out this period in detail, it would be but a repetition of the same things from year to year. Such incidents as are necessary to spin out the thread of the narrative and finish the portraiture of this good man, will be crowded into the concluding chapter.

CHAPTER XIV.

His mode of Traveling.—Excursion in Missouri, 1820.—His monthly circuit in Missouri and Illinois.—A night Adventure.—A Horseback Excursion.—Origin of Carrollton Church.—Faith and Prayer.—Interview with Rev. J. Going.—A "Standard" Sermon.—An Affectionate Embrace.—Comforts of Old Age.—Last Illness and Death.

One of the peculiar physical characteristics of Father Clark, even to old age, was his habit of walking. The ordinary mode of traveling for ministers and all other persons who journeyed, both men and women, was on horseback. Carriage roads were infrequent, and buggies, the vehicle of modern times for traveling, were seldom seen on these frontiers. Females rode on horseback to Kentucky and Tennessee, to see their friends, on journies from four to eight hundred miles. But Father Clark had some singular scruples against using a beast of burden; and to one of his personal friends he intimated a religious vow while on the circuit in Georgia, that so long as man oppressed his fellow man, he did not feel free to use a horse. He was never accustomed to the management of a horse, as every frontier man has been from childhood, and he felt unhappy, if not in real fear, while riding one. Hence in nearly every tour he made, he walked.

In the summer of 1820, he made a preaching tour through the Boone's Lick country to the extreme frontier settlement north side of the Missouri river, to a place called Blufften. There was Dr. B. F. Edwards, a Baptist, with his young family from Kentucky, who received him cordially. No preacher of the gospel had then gone thus far in the vast west. Only a few families had reached that remote position, then on the border of the Indian country. There he preached the gospel in a small log cabin, and not even crowded with all the families within several miles.

In the Boone's Lick country, as the central part of Missouri was then called, he found a number of Baptist families, who claimed affinity with the "Friends to Humanity," and aided them in forming themselves into a church connection. In going and returning, he preached almost daily, as he passed from settlement to settlement.

For ten years before his death, he made a regular circuit, monthly, extending from Fox creek on the Merrimac, twenty miles, west-south-west from St. Louis, round by Coldwater, where was the church to which his membership was attached, and of which he was pastor. There, and near the Spanish pond, a settlement farther east, he held meetings for two, and sometimes three days in succession. At one period he crossed the Mississippi at a ferry a short distance below the mouth of the Missouri. That ferry being stopped, he turned down the course of the river to St. Louis, and passed over on the ferry-boat there. His route then was through the Six-Mile prairie, where he had a regular preaching station. From thence he occasionally diverged to Edwardsville, but more frequently went up the American bottom to Upper Alton, thence to Lofton's prairie, Judge Brown's, near the Maconpin, Carrollton, and above Apple Creek to a settlement called Henderson's Creek, where he collected a small church. Returning, he would deviate from this route to visit other settlements, on the right or left, as occasion called. The whole distance on these routes and back to Fox creek, was about two hundred and forty miles, and in the excursion he preached from thirty to forty times.

Some three or four times each year he visited the churches and his friends in St. Clair, and Monroe counties. At that period a congregation could be gathered on any day of the week by timely notice.

The ferry-boat already noticed below the mouth of the Missouri, was destroyed in a flood, and the ferry not again established. Without knowing this, Mr. Clark started from the Spanish pond, intending to cross at this upper ferry, which would have been a gain of thirty miles. He was obliged to turn down to St. Louis. His appointment next day was at Judge Lofton's, sixteen miles above Alton. Resolute on fulfilling his engagements, though threescore and ten years had brought on him the infirmities of age, he made his way by St. Louis, and crossed the ferry about dark. In traveling along the muddy pathway, in thick darkness, twenty-four miles to Upper Alton, through the dense forest of the American bottom, he became fatigued, and was repeatedly compelled to rest, by leaning against a tree. He reached the hospitable family of a Presbyterian friend at breakfast. He was excessively fatigued, and on inquiry, the family were astonished to learn he had traveled the whole night and preceding day. Regarding such an effort as an undue sacrifice from a feeble old man, his hospitable friend ventured an admonition that he should not expose himself. He received a response in the mildest language and intonations of voice,—"O, my dear brother, souls are precious, and God sometimes uses very feeble and insignificant means for their salvation. The people expect me to fill my appointments, and the only way was to reach here this morning. This is nothing to what our divine Master did for us."

Mr. L., in rehearsing this incident, stated he felt humbled and rebuked at the patience, perseverance, and ceaseless energy of this old minister in the service of the Lord.57

He had walked eight miles to his customary crossing place on the river, thence eighteen miles to St. Louis, twenty-four miles to Upper Alton, and by two o'clock he was sixteen miles further, preaching to the congregation in Lofton's prairie. This made sixty-six miles walking in a muddy path, without sleep, so consciously strict was he to fulfill his engagements.

The spring and early summer of 1824, were unusually wet, the rain poured down from the clouds almost daily, the mud was deep in the paths, and it was exceedingly difficult and unpleasant on foot. His friends in Missouri furnished him a small, gentle horse, called a pony, put on him a new saddle, bridle and saddle-bags, and after much persuasion induced Mr. Clark to mount, and ride his customary circuit. He consented, and was placed on the ambling pony, and, much to the gratification of his friends, started on his journey. He was troubled lest the horse should hurt himself, or hurt him. At every creek, pond and slough, he dismounted, threw his saddle bags over his own shoulders, took off his nether garments, as he was accustomed to do when walking, and carefully led the horse through mud and water, often three feet deep. The care of the animal distracted his thoughts, and, on his return, he begged his friends to take back the horse and relieve him from a burden that seriously interfered with his religious and ministerial duties.

When Sunday schools, Bible societies, and missions were brought before the people on these frontiers, he entered at once into these measures, and threw his influence in that direction. He carried a small Bible, or two or three Testaments, in his little wallet to supply the destitute families he visited. He took a deep interest in the first seminary in these frontier States, and encouraged his brethren to coöperate in the good work.58

When the first periodical that advocated the interests of religion, education, and social organizations for philanthropic purposes, was published and circulated in his range, his influence gave it impulse. He not only circulated periodicals and tracts among the people, but read such publications in the families he visited, and impressed the subjects on the minds of his listening auditors, by familiar conversation.

In the vicinity of Carrollton, Ill., were a few Baptists from Vermont, New York, and Ohio, who were dissatisfied with the anti-mission, do-nothing policy of a class of Baptists that had a little church in that vicinity. Carrollton was the seat of justice for Greene county, and situated in the centre of a large farming population, and it was desirable to have a Baptist church organized there, without being impeded by the influence and prohibitions of the anti-mission party. To this station Father Clark devoted a portion of his labors. Meetings were held in the court-house, an unfinished wooden structure. Two males and five females having entered into covenant relation in church-fellowship, under the instruction and guidance of the pioneer preacher, a call was made on three preachers in St. Clair county, to visit the place, preach to the people, and give the hand of fellowship to these brethren as a church in gospel order.59

These ministers left the north side of St. Clair county on Friday morning, the 27th day of April, 1827. The weather was unpleasant, and a succession of showers continued through the day. They had to ride forty miles to reach Judge Lofton's, where they were to pass the night. Their breakfast place was twelve miles further on, at Judge Brown's residence. Another twelve miles would bring them to the place of meeting, and the time to commence was twelve o'clock on Saturday.

At night, when the party reached Judge Lofton's residence, the weather was most unfavorable. A thick, dark mantle covered the sky, and sent down a steady chilling rain. So it was at nine o'clock. The road had been quite muddy and the traveling unpleasant. The small streams that crossed their path began to rise, and might be in swimming order by morning. They lay down to rest with desponding expectations of reaching the appointment in season.

Next morning, as the first gleams of light glanced over the prairies, the party was up and on their horses. But what a change in the aspects of nature! The clouds were dispersed, the air was soft and exhilarating; and as the sun rose, with healing in his beams, and threw streams of light through the rain drops that glistened on every shrub; gold, emeralds, rubies and diamonds reflected their mingled hues on every side. Birds were celebrating their matins in every spray. The path was muddy, and the streams were at fording places past the mid sides of their horses, but these inconveniences were of too small moment to cause

109

uneasiness. The party dashed on with their high-spirited horses, and arrived at the cabin of their hospitable friend, Judge B—— just as the coffee, corn-cakes, chickens, and other edibles, smoking hot, were ready for the table. The party, both men and horses, were soon refreshed, and being reinforced by a dozen or more persons on their way to the meeting, they proceeded. Just at the time of high noon they entered the village of Carrollton, and made their way across the open area, left for the public buildings, to the house of a Baptist minister,[60] who lived for the time being in the village where they knew the pioneer preacher would be found. He was standing in the door-way, and as his eye caught a glimpse of the ministers, he stepped out; his head was bare and his silvered locks gently agitated by the balmy breeze. The sun shone in meridian splendor, and every thing in nature was a type of the calm and joyous spirit that reigned within. Seizing the hands of his three brethren in the ministry, he exclaimed with the pious ejaculation,—"Bless the Lord, O my soul, and forget not all his benefits. I knew you would come. I prayed for you all day yesterday until I got an answer; and I felt strong in the faith the clouds would disperse, and we should have fair weather and a good time."

The unexpected change of the weather had been a topic of conversation by the party during their morning's ride, and one remarked, "I should not be surprised to learn that Father Clark has been praying for us."

We leave it to that class of speculatists, who fancy that the Almighty does not concern himself with human affairs, to explain the philosophy of this sudden and unexpected change. Doubtless they can solve the mystery by referring to an occult female, without either intelligence, goodness, or power, called NATURE, by whose LAWS every change is produced. Their progenitors lived about 3,680 years ago, and in their superabundant wisdom exclaimed, *"What is the Almighty that we should serve him; and what profit should we have if we pray unto him."*[61]

The little church in Carrollton received the fellowship of the brethren, and was visited by Father Clark nearly every month, while he was able to travel, while Mr. Dodson, who lived in that county several years, furnished occasional aid. The mystical number of seven members remained, but the fallow ground was broken up, the seed was sown in the congregation, and the year before his death, when he could no longer walk the long circuit of two hundred and forty miles, the spirit of the Lord was poured out, and large accessions were made. He labored in faith, prayer and feebleness, and other men gathered in the harvest.

The year 1831 was signalized by the visit of the late Rev. Jonathan Going to this valley. He spent some time in Illinois, and Father Clark heard of him, and so arranged as to meet him at the first annual session of the Edwardsville Association. The writer had given Mr. Going some outline of his character, labors and peculiarities. Each was desirous to hear the other preach. The congregation was unusually large for that period, especially on Sabbath. It was mid-summer, the weather hot, and the people were provided with rough seats, under the trees, adjacent to Upper Alton, and not many yards from the present site of Shurtleff College. Two and three discourses were then listened to with interest and patience at one sitting. The meeting continued without intermission for about four hours. The people gathered from fifteen and twenty miles distant, and would return the same day. No one was fastidious of the dining hour, or cared a straw for the conventionalities of a higher civilization. Mr. Clark had several peculiar sermons, not on paper, for he never used notes;—but in his mind, one of which he would draw forth on such occasions, and preach to large and Christian audiences. One had the text from one of the prophets, and the imagery of the STANDARD, or military ensign, under which the cohorts were marshalled.

Allusion was had, prophetically, to the army of Christ in the gospel day. In his illustrations he referred to the order in the army of Israel, as given in the first and second chapters of Numbers, and their march, each tribe under its own banner. The application of the figure was made to the various denominational forms of organic Christianity. Each standard had its appropriate emblem.

The Protestant Episcopal cohort had inscribed on their liturgical standard, *"Let all things be done decently and in order."*

The Presbyterians inscribed, *"And ye, fathers, provoke not your children to wrath, but bring them up in the nurture and admonition of the Lord."*

The Methodists hoisted their banner, with letters of fire,—*"Work out your own salvation with fear and trembling."*

The Baptists had on their flag, which they held with great tenacity,—*"To the law and to the testimony; if they speak not according to this word, it is because there is no light in them."*

Under each head he touched on the peculiarities of each sect, and showed that each held a portion of divine truth, and did valiant service in the army of Prince Emanuel.

There was just enough of quaintness and eccentricity in this mode of preaching the gospel to keep every one wide awake, and cause every hearer to remember and "inwardly digest" what he heard. Few men would crowd into a sermon more evangelical thoughts, or make more vivid and happy illustrations.

The old pioneer was not less interested in the impressive sermon of Mr. Going on missions, and the wonderful progress made in the work of translating and publishing the Scriptures, and preaching the gospel to the heathen.

At the close of such exhilarating meetings, a lively hymn is sung, and the friendly grasp of the hand of christian fellowship extended through the highly excited congregation.

Brethren crowded towards the stand to reach the hand of the "strange brother," who had so opportunely appeared in the "Far-West." Some one called on him to come down from the platform, where all the people could approach him.

Father Clark, whose day of discharge every one knew could not be far distant, approached with light in his eyes and joy in his countenance. He first seized one hand with a nervous grasp, then the other; then struck both palms on his shoulders, and before there was time to reflect, threw both arms around his body with an affectionate embrace, and gave him the ancient salutation on both cheeks. The vast congregation were melted, and many voices became so tremulous that the singing almost ceased.

But "the end of all things is at hand." The friends of Father Clark saw the infirmities of age pressing on him. His walks were limited, his preaching less frequent, and his visits to families were fewer and at longer intervals.

He had gained a home in every family he visited, and a place in every Christian heart. There was no murmuring; nor fretfulness; no complaining of the degeneracy of the age, which is the common failing of old men.

His friends gave him money whenever he needed it. He was seldom known to have a larger sum than fifty cents at one time, and then he felt uneasy until he found some deserving object of charity to relieve him. He desired nothing, sought nothing, and needed nothing of this world's wealth. His wants were few and promptly supplied by his friends. He had every comfort he desired. He lived among a people where hospitality is a cardinal virtue, and the kind feelings of his friends were exhaustless.

Knowing his increasing infirmities, the author made an effort to visit him at William Patterson's house on Coldwater, but found he had gone to another home on Fox Creek, and pressing engagements prevented going there. The pen was substituted for a personal interview, and a sketch of his eventful life was commenced, but failing strength prevented its completion.62

He lingered along, growing more and more feeble until the autumn of 1833. A letter from one of his brethren, with whom he always found a hospitable and comfortable home,63 written to his friends in Illinois after his decease, tells the story of his decline in a few words.

"For two years before his death, he had been in a bad state of health, but still traveled through the settlements (St. Louis county) and preached till the 22d of September, when he preached his last sermon at the house of Mr. Quick. He was seized with a severe bowel complaint, which lasted several days, but from which he partially recovered.

"As in health so in his sickness, he must be traveling. We moved him four times in his sickness. On Friday morning, he breathed his last at the house of Elisha Patterson."

This we suppose to be the 11th of October, 1833. Had he lived to the 29th of November, he would have attained seventy-five years.

His funeral was attended the next day by a large concourse of people. It is not known that he had a relative on earth living, but the Christian people over the whole country where he preached were his sincere mourners.

His mortal remains were deposited in a burying ground, on which the church, with which he lived and died, had erected a house of worship of hewn logs, and his friends placed at the head and foot of his grave a pair of neat marble tombstones, with a suitable inscription.

The place is now an obscure one, out of sight from all public roads. A lot has been provided by a liberal and philanthropic gentleman of St. Louis for the special purpose of a resting place for the Pioneer Preachers of Missouri. Thither it is proposed to convey the remains of FATHER CLARK, THE PIONEER PREACHER.

APPENDIX.

In the "Western Christian Advocate," Cincinnati, of October, 1834, we found a communication from Rev. John Glanville, the circuit preacher of the Methodist Episcopal Church, in St. Louis county, dated Sept. 25th, from which we give the following extract, relating to Mr. Clark.

"The first preacher that brought the gospel, as understood and taught by the Methodists, across the mighty Mississippi, was the Rev. John Clark. While this country was under the Spanish Government, it was an *illegal* act;—but not in reference to that *law* which makes the minister of God a debtor to the Jew and to the Greek; to the wise and the unwise. Having received a commission to preach the gospel to every creature, God sent him not on a warfare at his own cost. Seals to his ministry yet remain in this circuit.

"I saw him on his death-bed. He insisted on being taken to the meeting place. It was done. He enjoyed himself under preaching. Class meeting followed. The old man seemed like a person returned to his home and his friends like a long absence, exulting, rejoicing, and declaring that for many years he had been subject to doubts about his acceptance with God; but that for fours years past, he had not a doubt, and was calmly waiting for his departure. The next time I came to the place, I laid him in the tomb. He had returned to the same house to be at meeting, but on the preceding day was called to the great assembly above."

FUNERAL DISCOURSES.

It has been customary throughout the south and west to preach funeral discourses, after interment, at such time as may accommodate the largest number of friends or relatives. Rev. Messrs. James and Joseph Lemen had been selected by Mr. Clark for this purpose. After conferring with those more directly concerned, the following places were selected, and due notice given in the papers.

Bethel meeting-house in St. Clair county, the first Sabbath in February;—New Design, in Monroe county, second Sabbath;—Judge Brown, in Greene county, on the third Sabbath;—and Coldwater in Missouri, at William Patterson's, the fourth Sabbath in February. It was stated in the notice,—"The object in preaching at these several places, is to afford opportunity to the friends of our deceased Father to join in paying this last tribute of respect to his worthy memory. These places furnish central localities in the great moral vineyard, where his labors were ordinarily bestowed." Immense congregations attended these appointments.

FOOTNOTES

1 The true aboriginal name of the MISSISSIPPI.

2 Prov. xxiii: 5.

3 Transport ships are engaged in carrying soldiers and munitions of war from one country to another.

4 1 Cor. xv: 33.

5 Eccl. vii: 14.

6 A convoy is one or more ships of war sent to protect merchant vessels and transports.

7 Technically "burst."

8 A Letter of Marque is a merchant vessel, licensed to go armed, and fight in defense in time of war.

9 A cartel is an agreement between nations at war, for exchange of prisoners. It is also used for the vessel that brings them home.

10 They proved to be the captain and two mates of the vessel.

11 Jer. x: 23.

12 Job xxviii: 28.—Ps. cxi: 10.—Prov. i: 7; ix: 10; xv: 33.—Luke xii: 5.

13 Job xvi: 2.

14 Ezek. xviii: 20.

15 Luke xviii: 13.

16 Acts ix: 6.

17 Psalmist, H. 472.

18 Rom. viii: 14–17.

19 1 Cor. xii: 3.

20 2 Peter iii: 18.

21 Looking into the History of the Methodist Episcopal Church, by Rev. Dr. Bangs, Vol. 1, p. 253, we find the following under 1786.

"At the Conference in Virginia, a proposal was made for some preachers to volunteer their services for the State of Georgia, and several offered themselves for this new field of labor. Two of those who offered themselves, namely, Thomas Humphries and John Major, were accepted, and they went to work in the name of the Lord, and were made a blessing to many. They formed a circuit along settlements on the banks of the Savannah river, round by Little river, including the town of Washington. During the year they formed several societies, containing upwards of four hundred members—so greatly did God bless their labors."

117

The preceding year (1785) Thomas Humphries was on Tar river circuit, N. C., and John Major on Mecklenburg circuit in Virginia. Very probably the emigration of Methodists from his circuit to Broad river in Georgia, drew him there.

22 Conference Minutes, vol. 1, pp. 39 and 41.

23 Many of our readers require telling that *Episcopal hierarchies* have what they call three "*Orders*" in the ministry, in ascending grades; as, *deacons, presbyters* or *priests*, and *bishops*. The last named communicates the official gift to those below him, by "laying on of hands." The Methodist Episcopal Church has the same orders, though in a modified form. With them the term Elder is used to express the second grade.

24 Minutes, Vol. 1, p. 20.

25 Psalmist—Hymn 1068.

26 We give old English names for these garments, purposely; such as they were called before finical and apish people changed them for the unintelligible ones now used.

27 Bib. Antiq., vol. I., Chap. V., pp. 115–129. Amer. S. S. Union.

28 1 Cor. ix: 19–23.

29 1 Cor. i: 30.

30 37 1-2 cents.

31 Butternut—*Juglans alba oblonga.*

32 The edition before us is the seventh, and "printed by John Dunlap, at the newest printing office in Market street, Philadelphia, MDCCLXXIII." [1773.] The title page reads, "A Confession of Faith, put forth by the Elders and Brethren of many Congregations of Christians, (Baptized upon Profession of their Faith,) in London and the Country."

Adopted by the Baptist Association, met in Philadelphia, Sept. 25, 1742. This "Confession" had its origin in fact from "seven congregations gathered in London, 1643," and revised and adopted by "Ministers and Messengers of upwards of one hundred baptized congregations in England and Wales," in 1689. The "Confession" of that year is signed by thirty-eight persons, as a committee, "in the name and behalf of the whole assembly." The name of the renowned Hanserd Knollys stands at the head of the committee. The object of this Confession, was not to have a "standard," or rule of faith, separate from or in addition to the Scriptures, in the churches, but "for the satisfaction of all other Christians that differ from us in the point of baptism."

33 Job xxxviii: 2.

34 At that period (1796,) the Methodists had five circuits in Kentucky, ten preachers in the traveling connection, and 1880 whites and 64 blacks in their societies. Their preachers, learning that Mr. Clark had left the Methodist connection, gave him no direct encouragement as a preacher. Mr. Jolliff, Rev. J. Lillard, and two or three other preachers were Independent Methodists, and affiliated with Clark.

According to Asplund's Register, there were 57 Baptist churches, 50 ordained ministers, 16 licentiates, and 3,453 members, in 1792. Twenty per cent. increase at least should be added for their number in 1796. This would give 4,150 communicants.

35 Pictures.

36 It will not be thought strange that such a boy as Thomas Bush (which is a fictitious name for a real personage) became a graduate of Transylvania University, studied law in Lexington, was elected to Congress, and became a Judge of the Court. In all these stations he was an honor to himself, and to those who trained him for usefulness and respectability. He also became a Christian professor, lived a life of faith in Jesus Christ, and died in the full hope of a blessed immortality.

37 Whiskey in which cherries have been steeped.

38 This is the aboriginal meaning of Mississippi.

39 Their towns were situated about twenty miles a little east of north from Springfield, and not far from where now the Chicago and Mississippi railroad crosses Salt Creek, in Logan county. Kickapoo, a branch of Salt Creek, may be seen on the sectional map of Illinois.

40 The cordelle is a long rope attached to the bow of the boat, and drawn over the shoulders of the men, who walk along the bank. The setting-pole is about ten or twelve feet long, with the lower end shod with iron, and the upper end terminating in a knob, which is pressed against the shoulder, and the men who use them walk forwards on the narrow gunwale, in a very stooping posture, with their faces towards the stern. This shoves the boat against a strong current. When the hands on the gunwale next the shore drop their poles and catch hold of limbs and bushes that overhang the river and pull the boat forward, it is called "bush-whacking." Oars are used in crossing the river from one shore to the other. A long heavy oar with a wide blade is attached to the stern so as to move on a pivot, and the steersman, who is commandant for the occasion, directs the boatmen. This was the mode of ascending western rivers before the "Age of Steam."

41 A species of New England rum, brought from New Orleans.

42 James Lemen, Sen., became a Baptist preacher, and died January 8th, 1823. He left four sons in the ministry, all of whom, venerable men, are still living in 1854.

43 Judge Martin's History of Louisiana, vol. ii, p. 90.

44 Ibid, p. 153.

45 Stoddard's Sketches of Louisiana, pp. 211–224. Annals of the West; St. Louis Edition, 1850, p. 543. The aggregate population of Upper Louisiana at the period of the cession, was about 10,120, of which 3,760 were French, including a few Spanish families; 5,090 were Anglo-Americans, who had come into the country after 1790;—and 1,270 black people, who were slaves, with a few exceptions. Indians were not counted, although several bands had their villages within the bounds of the settlements.

46 The Spanish prison. Jail.

47 This is *Fife* in French orthography, and the name of a Frenchman who first settled on it.

48 *Clo-shai*—a steeple.

49 Robert Lemen, Esq., of St. Clair county, Illinois.

50 Rev. Joseph Lemen, *ibid.*

51 Rev. James Lemen, then junior, now senior.

52 For about twenty years, we depend wholly on the recollections of his surviving friends, for the incidents of his life and labors. The facts have been obtained, but after protracted and diligent search, we cannot in all cases accurately fix the dates. In no instance do we vary from the exact period more than four or five years.

53 Red Staff, from the color of the flag-staff.

54 Rev. James Lemen, who narrated the incident to the author.

55 We extract the following correspondence from the WESTERN PIONEER, of which the author was editor, of February 16, 1831.

"The following letter from Judge Brown to the editor will be read with pleasure by many of our subscribers. The venerable Father Clark has long been known in Illinois and Missouri as a prudent, but uncompromising advocate of human freedom and the rights of man. The ladies could not have paid the worthy father in the ministry a happier compliment than making him a member of the Colonization Society.

CARROLLTON, Ill., December 25, 1830.

DEAR SIR:—The cause of Colonization is gaining ground in our county, and many, both male and female, take a deep interest therein. The Rev. John Clark was constituted a life member of the auxiliary society of Greene County, on the 12th inst., by the patriotic ladies of Lofton's prairie and its vicinity, who is the first person, so far as I know, who has been constituted by the ladies a member of that most benevolent institution. I hope for the honor of those ladies, and to stimulate others to follow the example they have set, you will publish the following resolution, with such remarks as you may deem proper to promote the cause of colonization, which I consider a most efficient means that ever have been adopted to civilize and Christianize the uncultivated and barbarous tribes of Africa, as well as to wipe away a foul stain from our national character.

Respectfully your obedient servant, JEHU BROWN.

CARROLLTON, Ill., Dec. 25, 1830.

At a called meeting of the Auxiliary Colonization Society of Greene county, it was

Resolved, That the thanks of this society be presented to the ladies of Lofton's prairie and vicinity, for their generosity and benevolent feelings in constituting Rev. John Clark a life member of this society.

By order of the President. MOSES O. BLEDSOE, Secretary.

56 The author tried the practice of bathing the feet in cold water in the morning, while traveling on these frontiers, and found it invariably injurious to *him*. The application of cold water to the feet and body of more than one-fourth is positively injurious. To others it is highly beneficial. This depends on the *temperament*. Mr. Clark had a sanguine-nervous temperament, and received benefit. The writer has a bilious-nervous temperament, and the circulation sluggish. To such, the experience and observation of fifty years have taught that the cold bath is injurious, while the hot bath is exhilarating. Careful observation and experience are the only safe guides. It is sheer quackery to prescribe the same treatment to all persons.

57 This was Enoch Long, Esq., now of Galena, Ill.

58 This was the seminary at Rock Spring, which proved the embryo of Shurtleff College.

59 This is the usage amongst Baptists. No ecclesiastical authority is required to constitute a church. Any number of the disciples of Christ, when baptized on a profession of faith, can unite in church fellowship. Ministers and other brethren, on invitation, meet with them, and give them public recognition as being in union.

60 Rev. Elijah Dodson.

61 Job xxi: 15.

62

COPY.—Coldwater, Mo., Sept. 20th, 1832.

DEAR FATHER IN THE GOSPEL:

I have come this way on my tour to the Missouri Association, with the hope of seeing you, and having one more interview on the shore of time. I imagine you have gotten to the banks of Jordan, and are waiting for the boat to carry you safely across.

I have some special business with you, on behalf of your friends, which I meant to have done by word of mouth, but now must do it with the pen. During your long pilgrimage, you have been *trying to do good*, and no doubt wish to keep *trying* the inch of time you may remain with us. Some of your Christian friends are anxious you should do some *good on earth*, after you have joined the ranks above.

Your friends think a memoir of your life, including your conversion, experience, travels, and labors would be interesting and useful to the living; and they are not willing to part with you without having the materials left.

Your labors in this country are intimately connected with the religious history of the country, and to have an accurate account of the one, we must have a sketch of the other. We wish you to commence writing, the mere facts and dates, without regard to style, soon, and continue as your strength permits. Yours with due respect,

63 Mr. William Patterson.